SMILLA'S SENSE OF SNOW

The Making of a Film by Bille August
Adapted from the Novel by Peter Høeg

Karin Trolle

THE NOONDAY PRESS 97
FARRAR, STRAUS AND GIROUX
NEW YORK

The following chapters have been translated into English
by Barbara J. Haveland:

- Preface
- Film Must Speak to the Heart:
  A Conversation between Peter Høeg and Bille August
- Theater Director Simon Løvstrøm:
  Greenlanders in Denmark and Danes in Greenland
- From Copenhagen to Greenland: Filming on Location
- The Ice Cave, the *Kronos*, and the White Palace:
  Setting the Scene for *Smilla*
- Interviews with Agga Olsen and Clipper Miano

Illustrations: Copyright © Constantin Film Produktion GmbH
except
pages 9, 12, 17, 23, and 28: Copyright © Joakim Ladefoged/PolFoto
Stills photographer: Rolf Konow
and
pages 150, 153, 158, 163 (TOP), 164, 165 (BOTTOM): Ole Kragh-Jacobsen
Storyboards: Simon Bang
except
page 73: Carl Aldana
Scenographic drawings: Love Malmsten
Layout and type setting: Jan Birkefeldt Andersen
Cover design: Tegnestuen/Harvey Macaulay
Printed by Nordgraf A/S

Published simultaneously in Canada by HarperCollins*CanadaLtd*

Printed in Denmark

First edition, 1997

Library of Congress catalog card number: 96-072250

Preface

As you sink back into your cinema seat and find yourself becoming captivated by Julia Ormond's fascinating portrayal of Smilla; as you marvel at the breathtaking scenery of Greenland gliding past up there on the screen and are carried away by the drama being enacted around the murder of a small boy, you do not—nor should you—give any thought to the fact that behind those thrilling two hours in the darkened cinema lie months of concentrated work on the part of a great many people.

You hope to become so caught up in the story itself that you never stop to wonder where on earth the money was found for such a huge project, how Bille August and Julia Ormond managed to create such an enthralling female character, or how difficult it must have been to shoot takes on an ice floe in Greenland at temperatures of twenty degrees below freezing.

This book represents an attempt to provide some small insight into the process of making a film. An artistic process in which—owing to a tight schedule and various practical considerations—the director, the cameraman, the set designer, and the cast are not always working under absolutely optimum conditions. An operation in which allowances have to be made for all sorts of practical and technical details and which must be organized more or less along the lines of a military exercise. But, above all, a thoroughly enjoyable and inspiring process in which every task is carried out amid the most tremendous esprit de corps and the sense of a common commitment, with but one aim in mind: that the film the general public will eventually see will be every bit as good as it possibly can be.

Karin Trolle

Contents

Part Three

Part One

Film Must Speak to the Heart: A Conversation between Peter Høeg and Bille August

Interview with Jes Stein Pedersen

*B*ille is still suffering from jet lag after a flight from the other side of the globe. Peter's cheeks are rosy, his hair windswept after a bike ride from his row house in Copenhagen. Over the next couple of hours, for two of Denmark's most successful artists the focus is once more on Smilla Jaspersen, that extraordinary character with whom both have been so deeply involved. Peter created her; Bille transferred her to the silver screen. She started out as a feeling inside Peter not long after the birth of his first child, and as a fully formed fictional character she took the whole world by storm. After a run through Bille's image workshop the half-Inuit woman with the keen eye and a fierce sense of justice is now about to take on the world of motion pictures. Not quite five years separates the initial Danish publication date of Smilla's Sense of Snow *from the date when the film goes on general release.*

This interview *brings together* two artists, *both of whom are exceptionally capable of reflection, to explain for the first time what they would like us to discern in the headstrong, superintelligent, fascinating woman from icebound, crime-ravaged Copenhagen, a city shrouded in mystery.*

Bille, what went through your head the first time you encountered Smilla?

Bille: Smilla is a quite exceptional character: vulnerable, complex, divided, profound, and astute. By the time I'd read the first thirty pages of the novel I knew that I was part of Smilla and that I wanted to have even more to do with her. I was totally hooked; I knew straight away that this unique story of Peter's would make a tremendous film.

When his publisher contacted me I must have been the only Dane not to have read the book. It was just about to be published in the States, and thirty film companies from all over the world had already applied to buy the film rights. I felt greatly honored and very touched to find that there was some interest in involving me in the project. I jumped at the chance.

I have always been fascinated by stories involving human beings with nothing to lose—like Smilla, very early on in the book, when she returns to the apartment house where she lives to find perhaps the only person she loves dead. This puts her in a very vulnerable position. Everyone says it was an accident, but her instinct tells her she's dealing with murder. We can tell that something very big and very sinister is afoot and that Smilla will have to keep going to the bitter end in order to find out who murdered the boy and why. Not out of revenge but quite simply so that her life can once more make sense.

It is a wonderfully exciting opening. The reader *has* to know what happened. And along the way we're presented with a host of marvelous cameos of people in the civilized nation of Denmark and with the quite distinctive view of our way of life which is Smilla's—half-Dane, half-Greenlander as she is—by virtue of her foreignness. A fine yet dreadful portrait of modern society. One is struck by Smilla's clear-sightedness. Especially as a Dane, since the majority of us have a bad conscience about the way we have treated the Greenlanders since the early 1950s, when we decided to turn Greenland into a modern society without asking its inhabitants first.

A WONDERFUL SITUATION

Peter, you're not a great filmgoer and you don't own a television set. What did you think when you heard that your book was suddenly to be brought to life on film and that Bille was to have the job of effecting this transformation?

Peter: I thought what a wonderful situation this presented. It's not often that one has both a Danish book with impact and a great Danish director who is capable of orchestrating the machinery necessary to make it into a film. One might have expected that you, Bille, would make only films based on screenplays produced abroad, that being the usual source of everything that ends up on film.

I thought there was a synchronicity about it that was quite beautiful.

Where did you start? How much discussion was there between the two of you about the screenplay?

Bille: The first time we met, it was just for a brief chat, to see whether we had the same story in mind. That was the most crucial meeting. It didn't last all that long. We immediately realized that we shared the same view of the story and how to put it over on film. That was the main thing. If we had seen things differently we would have had to go our separate ways and someone else would have had to make the film. Fortunately, we were absolutely on the same wavelength.

Peter: As I remember it, there were three things we talked about. First of all, the film would have to respect the book's subtly shifting view of Greenlanders. I have tried my best to render it unsentimental. There are so many ridiculously romanticized images of the Third and Fourth Worlds which completely forget the harshness that characterizes living conditions in such places. We were totally in agreement on that point.

The second thing we discussed was that the film would have to respect the feminine outlook of the central character. I know from your other films, Bille, that you have never betrayed any of your female characters; nevertheless, I wanted to have a word with you about it. When men make films with a woman in the leading role one is often faced with an

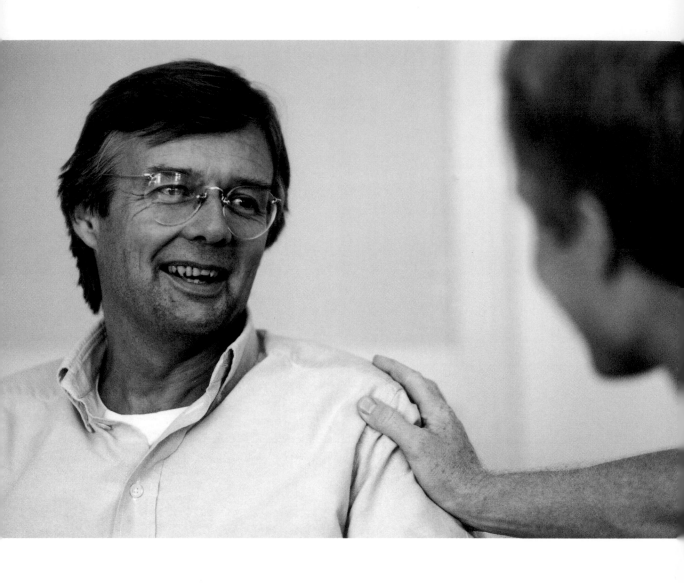

extremely subtle form of pornography, with the camera pandering to the male point of view every chance it gets; in other words, being employed in a pornographic fashion.

As far as your images of women are concerned, Bille, it really is almost as if you were a woman yourself! You must have a very good grasp of the feminine side of your own nature.

The third thing I said, right at the outset, was that Bille must not feel in any way tied to the book; that a literal cinematic translation of the book was of no interest. Much better, then, that Bille should be inspired by some resonance, or some quality, in the book.

DISASTROUS SCREENPLAY

The novel, which is at once a thriller, an account of a psychological rite of passage, and a merciless critique of the civilized world, has its roots in Smilla's own inner monologue. Did you have much of a struggle in transforming such a complex book into a film everyone can understand?

Bille: We got in touch with an American scriptwriter, who then came over to Denmark. We had a number of meetings, also involving Peter, and went into every aspect of the story in great depth. The scriptwriter was incredibly well prepared. He knew the book ten times better than either Peter or I did. After we had all three reached agreement on what was to form the core of the film, the scriptwriter and I carried on without Peter. Unfortunately, the first screenplay was awful, an absolute disaster. So I had to start all over again. *Smilla* used up four scriptwriters before we managed to get the two universes to meld: the outer framework—the action as such, that is—and the portrayal of Smilla. It cost a lot of dollars.

What was the problem?

Bille: The structure of the novel is exceptionally sophisticated. Converting that into something as concrete as film is extremely difficult. The actual thriller side is not all that difficult, although it does present its own difficulties. But it was Smilla who presented the biggest problem or, if you like, the greatest challenge. Producing a credible image of her, of her complexity, her clarity and depth—that was a really tough assignment. The novel is written in the first person. Smilla is highly intelligent and very philosophical and has a most intriguing outlook on life, but there is no way that this can be transferred directly onto film. Transcribing her thoughts into concrete set pieces would bring with it the risk that she would come over as a pain in the neck, a know-it-all. We knew we didn't want to work with a voice-over, i.e., a narrator. There is no way one can convert her thoughts from the book into actual dialogue in the film. Transferring Smilla's inner universe and inner life onto film gave us our biggest headache.

What was it that finally caused the screenplay to fall into place?

Bille: It's an instinctive thing. I can't say exactly when or how it happened. You can sense when a screenplay is perfect, when it rings true. What I was after was that very special air of unease that pervades the book; that weird, steel-gray, and deadly world which this astonishing woman inhabits. Not until very late in the scriptwriting process did I start to rediscover the mood I knew had to be there if the film was to be successful.

If you are too unnerved by a book's celebrity or its greatness, to the point where you stick too literally to it, it will always turn out badly. Personally, I feel that the underlying mood in *Smilla* the film comes pretty close to that of the book.

AN OBSCURE ENDING

The novel has a rather obscure ending. Peter, I know you've had some reservations about its conclusion. Have you learned anything from seeing the book turned into a film that must have a clearly defined plot and a clear-cut conclusion?

Peter: One of the first things you told me, Bille, was that the ending in the book could not be used in a film. And I agree. I wrote a very literary ending, and there are several reasons for this. When I wrote the book I was aware that I was also working with certain stereotypes. In order to make contact with very deep-seated forces in people and capture their attention you have to work with certain emotions that are buried deep inside us. The atrocity committed against the child, man and woman, good and evil, archetypes of that type. Having worked with such profound symbolism throughout the book, I wanted, at the end, to reveal this to the reader by having the realistic plane of the novel crack. What have we here? Are we inside the mind of the author? Is this simply a psyche making its presence felt, the characters merely slivers of this psyche? What's going on? Doubt of this sort, put very simply here, can be engendered in books without the reader's feeling cheated. With film, it's another matter entirely.

Then there's the fact that it takes most people about a week to read the book. Reading nonstop would take you at least twenty-four hours. But with a film you have only two hours to work with. We command the viewer's attention for just one tenth of the narrative time demanded by the book. This fact changes everything. This is paramount when it comes to the narrative devices. That was one of the first things Bille told me, and I could understand that.

We toyed, though only for a second or two, with the idea of my trying to write the screenplay, but I didn't want to. I was tempted, because it would also have given me the chance to work with Bille . . .

Bille: We'll do that some other time.

Peter: Yes, we will. At that time I didn't know whether my system could take it. When you've been growing strawberries in the same bed for four years, then it's time to switch to another crop. *The Woman and the Ape* was already running through my mind. I couldn't go back into Smilla's world. Now I could have, because now I'm distanced from it. To your question as to what I have learned I would say that when I saw Bille's film I felt that I actually could write a film script. If I set aside six months and saw 150 films and thought it through very carefully I might well be able to put my mind to it. That's what I have learned. That there is in fact a greater similarity between the scriptwriter and the novelist than I had imagined.

I HEAR WORDS

Your writing style has been described as very cinematic, very visual . . .

Peter: I don't see in pictures. If my writing is cinematic it is more because anyone who says this has dug right down to those levels that film and fiction have in common. I see no pictures.

Bille: It's interesting that you should say that, because it comes across differently. When I read a scene from one of your books I have the impression that you've had a picture in mind and then described whatever you were seeing.

Peter: I hear words. Smilla was never really a person to me. She is a linguistic state—like a mask. A complicated mask, I grant you, and one that has to carry an entire novel, not a commedia dell'arte mask. She represents a distinct sensation in the body and in language, which I can enter. Especially while she was taking shape. There was never a picture. The first picture I saw of Smilla was on the dust jacket that was used throughout Europe of a skinny little woman standing on the ice with her back turned. All at once I saw how Smilla might look.

JULIA ORMOND IS UNIQUE

How do you think Julia Ormond has worked out as Smilla?

Peter: Perfectly satisfactory!

She isn't a translation of Smilla, nor should she be. She comes over as a unique personality with a great deal of Smilla's vulnerability and intelligence. It has taken me a surprisingly long time to get her out of my mind after seeing the film. I kept seeing her, but then I've experienced the same thing with all your films, Bille. That, to me, is where they differ from other films. There is a profound delicacy in the way you get the actors to play

their parts.

You feel that Bille has a good grasp of the feminine side of himself. In your books you also focus to a great extent on the feminine . . .

Peter: The Chinese school of philosophy may well be right in saying that inside every man there is a woman and that this is what he is searching for. Men yearn primarily, of course, after women in the external world, but underneath that there is an irresistible attraction toward a deeper, an elemental female quality that I'm sure I've tried to work toward in Smilla. The book might be said to be a sort of laboratory for research into femininity. The magical thing about the film Bille has made is that I feel that same pull toward the image of Smilla presented by the actress, Julia Ormond, as I feel toward that linguistic state inside myself which evolved into Smilla. Can you understand that? Smilla's vulnerability is incredibly important to me. Her sense of being alone in the world, where women generally find it easier to make themselves at home. Men find it simpler to be lone wolves. But Smilla possesses a vulnerability that makes it difficult for her to fit in. Ormond has caught that *so* well. There is a distinctive sensual quality about her that is so right. She is not torn intellectually and sensually; the two dovetail in a way that I see as being extremely un-Danish. Do you follow me?

Bille: That is precisely the approach Julia and I took to the part. Even though from a purely intellectual point of view she had always had a clear picture of Smilla's world, nonetheless Julia was faced with an enormous challenge in getting a credible performance out of Smilla.

The takes from the first week's filming had simply to be scrapped. Neither Julia nor I could come up with the right voice for Smilla. It's terribly difficult to bring out that bitterness and that detachment from other people, which derive from Smilla's clear-sightedness and her skeptical view of the world in which we live, without making her seem arrogant and superficial. In the takes from that first week she was a real bitch, with a haughtiness that could have proved disastrous had we not toned it down.

MAGIC IN FRONT OF THE CAMERA

As a filmgoer one is often at a loss to see how actors can play a part and make it look as though they have actually lived through the experiences, the pain, they are portraying on screen . . .

Bille: Leading actors, especially if they are in the situation of having to interpret an image as complex as that presented by Smilla for any length of time, may well tend to lose patience and overplay the character. My job, as the director, is to see to it that we leave some room for the viewer. When it comes to acting the audience plays a vital supporting role. The actors need to hold back a little. The members of the audience will themselves attribute a whole string of emotions to the characters in the piece. The actors don't have to do this. My job is to get the balance right.

Peter: There appear to be two trends in modern filmmaking, Bille. One of these involves leaving things more and more in the hands of the actors —especially the big stars, where the director counts on getting a far more convincing performance out of them by not interfering. I've just seen your film *The Best Intentions*, and to me the acting in that is unbelievably good, so fresh and with a totally understated sincerity. I can't even begin to imagine what must have gone on before the camera started to roll! There are some scenes of tremendous psychological complexity where the acting is such that one is totally taken in—it doesn't seem like acting at all . . . If you had spent too much time telling the actors what to do I can see how this could overtax their systems, so that they would be unable to act with the same sincerity and freshness. So the question is: How do you do it? How does one evoke such magic?

Bille: I love working with talented actors. I love forming relationships built on trust with good actors and creating some grand and convincing portraits. That, for me, is one of the greatest joys of filmmaking. What I am looking for when I read screenplays and books is the exposed—the naked—individual, pure feeling. If one can achieve that in a film, then I can think of no greater or finer form of drama. When I read *Smilla* my instinct told me it contained all the elements necessary for portraying, in partnership with some gifted actors, a group of people who really do have nothing to lose; for getting through to that naked, luminous soul. It starts as far back as that.

The actual work with the actors varies a great deal. Some take a very intellectual approach to their work and need you to talk to them at great length about the part. Others know exactly what's required. You only have to say a few words to them and right away they understand what it is you're looking for. Say too much to such an actor and he or she can get mad—really, they simply explode! Being a film director calls for great empathy. Some actors perform best in the second or third take, others are at their best in the tenth or eleventh. So obviously, if there is to be a cross-cut, I see to it that we first shoot the actor who works best in the early takes. You try to take advantage of the times when each is at his or her best. And after all, actors have to give of their best when the camera is on them—not during rehearsals or sometime later! It's a lengthy process in which timing counts, and that, to me, is the real fun part of filmmaking.

Peter: I think you have to see it in action to truly understand it. Sometime I'll have to watch you direct.

CAPTURED TO A T

Peter, has the film made any compromises that bother you—parts you would rather have seen cast differently?

Peter: No. I'm very surprised at how well the characters have been captured. I'd have thought it would be impossible to satisfy the author of the book. But that's not the case. All it takes is the necessary skill and the necessary wherewithal. In future I'm going to have a hard job separating many of the characters in the film from what I have written about them. Smilla is quite wonderful. Jakkelsen, from the ship, is a dead ringer for my own conception of him. The same goes for the pathologist. They may not look exactly as they are described in the book, but the inherent resonance of them, their human essence, is just as I envisaged it.

One thing about the film that I'm very happy with is the narrative pace that has been chosen, especially in the first two thirds of the film. It's quite different from the steady, epic drawing of breath that usually distinguishes Bille's films. As a matter of fact, in *Smilla* the action cuts from one scene to the next so fast that even I—who wrote the book—feel I really have to keep my wits about me. Certain things that time did not permit to be conveyed in words or in gestures have been assumed by many of the actors as subtle shades of their character. Smilla's father, for example. There are some very short scenes with Smilla, her father, and his woman friend, Benja. But much of the relationship between them is expressed through the way they hold themselves and the way in which the set design has shaped their surroundings.

FILM MUST SPEAK TO THE HEART

At one point in the book, Smilla refers with great fondness to Karl Marx's Das Kapital. *She speaks of its possessing "a trembling, feminine empathy" and a "potent indignation." On the whole she is very left-wing, and her criticism of society is pretty hard-hitting, not only because she is an outsider but also because she received her political education at the hands of a Greenland Marxist party. The novel contains quite a few analyses and assessments of life in the world today—as, for example, with our attitude toward time. That aspect of Smilla is not as pronounced in the film . . .*

Bille: Films speak directly to the heart; films transcend intellectual barriers. A film works if it stirs us emotionally, something that intellectual films rarely do. When we, as spectators, feel there is something in a film that is absolutely crucial, it is because it has spoken to our feelings. Whether Smilla quotes from Karl Marx or not is neither here nor there.

There is one scene in the film I'm particularly fond of. It's the one where she is having dinner with the Mechanic in his apartment, where she talks to him in such heartfelt terms about her love for mathematics. What she says is very beautiful and it links her own life and Greenland, while, through the Mechanic's eyes, we see her for the wonderful woman she is. For the first time in the film we are shown her fire and her passion, how committed she is. But at the same time she is ashamed that she has to give up investigating the boy's death for fear that her enemies will turn her claustrophobia against her. It's an extremely complicated monologue, but the scene works because it is seen more or less through the Mechanic's eyes. We see how warm she can be, what a deep person she is. It ends with his asking if he may kiss her. The point I want to make is that if this had been purely and simply a mathematics lecture, the scene would never have worked. But it *does* work, because of the emotional dimension. That, I believe, is the major difference between film and literature. Films speak directly to our emotions.

How do you feel about that, Peter?

Peter: The part about the outspoken criticism of society, that's one point on which the film differs from the book—but then it does contain something else not found in the book.

One of the things Bille said at the outset was that this film could never see the light of day as a Danish or a Scandinavian production. Simply fitting out the interior of the ship cost as much as the whole budget for a Danish feature film. The parts of the Danish characters in the book would have to be played by international actors—stars, all of whom have what Bille calls *screen presence*. Actors who shine no matter what part they may be playing. The element of Danish social realism that is a feature of the book cannot possibly be retained when you're making something intended for viewing by countless people all over the world. Deep down, I believe that that aspect can be understood only by Danes like ourselves and, at a pinch, by Norwegians and Swedes. There's no need to feel bad about it. The fact that the characters have to be transformed from their Danish nucleus into something else is simply a necessary condition.

If I couldn't have lived with that, I'd have had to say no; if Bille hadn't wanted to, *he* would have had to say no. Long before I could have known that the film of Smilla would turn out well, I knew that she would come

over with that special radiance all the great actors carry with them.

The social critique you're referring to can be fully understood only by us Danes and can be put over properly only if one is familiar with the world in which we live. Bille's film *The Best Intentions*—a film in which the social apprehension of a hierarchy is very clearly defined—can be fully understood only in a Scandinavian context, which is why it has not played to scores of millions of people but mainly to a limited audience in Scandinavia.

Bille: It is an exclusive product . . .

Peter: So one could say that something has been toned down or lost in the film. On the other hand, something else has been added that was not in the book. What has been created is a dreamlike Copenhagen, a city with a fairy-tale air to it. We see cars driving around and yet there is something mythical about the city. We know that isn't how it looks. It's awash with Poul Henningsen lamps and designer furniture. The film radiates something that is both archetypal and contemporary, a particular quality the book cannot provide in quite the same way. This is just one example of how the film takes a different tack and is able to offer something different in a way that seems to me to fill the bill.

A GOOD SENSE OF SNOW

The film was shot in Copenhagen, northern Sweden, and Greenland. It abounds in snow. How dependent were you on the weather, Bille?

Bille: When the film was still at the planning stage we hoped for just a little snow in Copenhagen. As it turned out, we had five hard winter months of snow and ice. There hadn't actually been a really cold winter since the year we made *Pelle the Conqueror*, so I guess I must be lucky when it comes to snow. We started shooting very late in the winter, in March, but it was bitterly cold and we had masses of snow. We only had to produce a little artificial snow for the street scenes; the rest of the film is full of the genuine article.

I had great reservations about filming in Greenland, thanks to the bad conscience I mentioned earlier. Any pictures I had seen of Greenland had all been along the lines of bleak street scenes in Nuuk. Then we arrived at the area where we did the location filming, Ilulissat on Disko Bay, and it was one of the most fantastic, most spectacular sights I'd ever seen. Majestic. The sense that here was a landscape totally untouched by the hand of man; the realization that the people who live there can never hope to alter the landscape but must live alongside it with the greatest humility —that is what has shaped the Greenlanders, given them their beautiful temperament and formed their bond with the natural world.

I understood Smilla much better once I had been to Greenland: her primordial force, her unsentimental clarity.

Had you visited Greenland before you wrote the book, Peter?

Peter: Yes, I had, but I don't know nearly as much about Greenland as might appear from the book. That's the way with writers. They cannot know a lot *and* write books; so they have to give the impression of knowing something!

INTEREST IN THE INDIGENOUS PEOPLES

Nowadays a lot of interest is being shown in the so-called indigenous peoples. There are many who feel that the aboriginal peoples may still harbor some unspoiled germ of humanity from which we might learn something. Its fundamental literary qualities apart, the success of Smilla *has been explained by the fact that it homes in on this particular spirit of the times. And yet you, Peter, say that we must not romanticize the people of the Fourth World. What is it outsiders can see that we are blind to?*

Peter: I don't really regard the Greenlanders as being especially indigenous, as something unspoiled that might tell us something about how we once were. I've spent a large part of my life in non-Western societies, in the tropics mainly. Smilla is every bit as tropical as she is polar. I've spent a lot of time in Africa, in particular. When I go there I don't go around looking

Bille August

Bille August was born in Denmark in 1948. In the late sixties he attended Christer Strömholm's School of Photography in Stockholm, going on from there, in the early seventies, to the Danish Film School.

August worked as a cinematographer on fourteen movies and TV features, mainly in Sweden, before starting his directing career with films such as *In My Life* (1979), *Zappa* (1982), and *Twist and Shout* (1985). But it was *Pelle the Conqueror* (1987) that put August firmly on the map of the international movie world. In 1988 it was awarded the Palme d'Or in Cannes, and in 1989 it won the Academy Award and the Golden Globe as Best Foreign Language Film.

The distinguished Swedish director Ingmar Bergman chose Bille August to film the script he had written about his

for something indigenous. I look for and savor certain distinct human traits, and miss others that are to be found at home, in Denmark. I'm a human being whose fate it is to shift location at regular intervals and take pleasure in whatever makes each place what it is. If you look at the interest in material things, in wealth, and in the notion that everything can be controlled—the weather, our health, and death, which can be put off indefinitely, as long as we have enough hospitals—it could be compared to the swing of the pendulum out to its farthest point.

It also has something to do with the status which, at a psychological level, the ego and the individual occupy in our culture, by which I mean: I am a unique human being, totally distinct from everyone else, with the right, regardless of the cost to others, to grab as much happiness for myself as I possibly can. In the long run, I don't see that as being a valid standpoint. It has prevailed for centuries, from the Renaissance up to the present day, with a drastic upturn in this century. But it's just about to run out of steam, both at a psychological and at a material level. Clearly, it cannot continue.

Then I look around for other models, although I don't know that they are especially indigenous. Both the Africans and the Inuits have been very good at taking from our culture whatever they could use and discarding the rest. That might even be what I like best about them, this unsentimental knack of appropriating from civilization whatever you can use and then throwing away the rest. I look upon other cultures as constituting a sort of fund of ideas or a record of other possible ways of living that could be every bit as good as our own.

NOT LIKE HOLLYWOOD

At one point in the book, Smilla says that as a Greenlander one might well wear a wristwatch, but one would never dream of going by it. She comments on the European's horror of any lulls in the social intercourse; someone always has to be saying something. Comments of this sort, on our society, are instrumental in giving the novel its unique character, but it has not in fact been possible to make so much of them in the film . . .

Peter: One of the very things I like about your films, Bille, is their approach to time. You aren't afraid to let a scene come right to a standstill. In *Smilla*, where the hectic pace is very much a feature of the film, there is one scene where she comes home after the interrogation scene and asks what can be done for depression. That scene is given all the time it could possibly need, whereas in so many other films a horror of stillness makes them pump as much action as possible into every frame. You are detached from Hollywood in a way that is somehow subtly linked to Smilla's detachment from the society she inhabits in Denmark . . .

Bille: When the Americans who helped finance the film of *Smilla* saw it for the first time, they told us that, besides liking the story, they felt that the film's language set its own terms and had a quality all its own; and also, that there was a touch of the exotic about the the pace of the narrative. It's an interesting point. Despite the fact that the film had to be made in English and would cost $40 million, which immediately categorizes it as mainstream cinema, we felt it was important that we preserve the integrity and the rhythm of the novel; that we stay true to our brief and to the character of Smilla, while at the same time finding a universal cinematic form capable of appealing to a wide audience. You could easily produce a more intellectual, a more sophisticated film, but I think you would probably end up with a film designed for a very limited audience. The brilliant thing about Peter's novel is that it combines scope with depth. It is an intellectual book that also happens to be vastly entertaining. It's a book that people who are not in the habit of reading books love to read—which is why it has become a worldwide bestseller. What I wanted was to make a film which would still be different and exotic, but which would also possess the broad appeal of the book. I believe this film is different. It is not a Hollywood product.

parents. This film, *The Best Intentions*, won August a second Palme d'Or in 1992.

August also directed two episodes in George Lucas's TV series *The Young Indiana Jones Chronicle*.

The Danish director's first movie with an international cast was *The House of the Spirits* (1993), the adaption of Isabel Allende's bestselling novel, starring among others Meryl Streep, Glenn Close, Jeremy Irons, Antonio Banderas, and Winona Ryder. Like *Smilla's Sense of Snow,* this film was produced by Bernd Eichinger.

In 1995, August made the epic turn-of-century movie and TV series *Jerusalem,* based on the Swedish writer Selma Lagerlöf's novel.

In addition to the aforementioned major awards, Bille August's work has won him a number of prizes and awards both in and outside Europe.

Peter Høeg

Peter Høeg was born in 1957 in Denmark and followed various callings—dancer, actor, fencer, sailor, mountaineer—before he turned to writing.

Høeg's first novel, *The History of Danish Dreams,* was published in 1988, and the Danish reviews acclaimed him as the "foremost writer of his generation."

Then followed *Tales of the Night* (1990) and *Smilla's Sense of Snow* (1992). Smilla established Høeg's international reputation. It was translated into more than thirty languages and was rapturously received by critics and fellow authors all over the world. In the United States, it was chosen by both *Time* magazine and *Entertainment Weekly* as their best novel of the year, and it appeared on bestseller lists around the country for months, including eleven weeks on the

A HAPPY ENDING?

The film has a quite clear-cut ending. I read somewhere that you once said the film could have ended in half a dozen different ways, and that there was a point when you weren't sure that it should have a happy ending . . .

Bille: Smilla does not embark on that long and dangerous voyage to find out the nature of the scientific mission these men are on. She wants to know what happened to the boy. In his book, Peter is able to weave her thoughts on many things into the action itself as it unfolds, as, for example, on the ship when she is thinking of Isaiah. In the concrete idiom of the film it would be wrong to bring the story to an end there, in the cavern of ice, with the disclosure of the meteorite and the parasites, because these are not the point. The boy is the point. That is why we chose to rewrite a conversation between Smilla and Ravn that occurs early on in the book as a conversation with Tørk right at the end, in which we are presented with the solution to the whole murder mystery. The meteorite and the parasite crop up in the course of the detective work, but the whole crux of the matter is that Smilla confronts those responsible for the murder with the truth. I don't think it is either a happy ending or the opposite, but the story is brought to a conclusion.

THE METEORITE

The part about the worm can be hard to grasp, but it has something to do with the fact that the rock heats up water that would normally be cold, thus creating the perfect growth conditions for certain rather nasty parasites . . .

Bille: The cinemagoer needs to know why the bad guys found it necessary to take the lives of others in order to achieve their goal. Loyen's and Tørk's goal is fame, scientific acclaim. The boy fell foul of them because he knew what had taken place back when his father died. They keep an eye on him because he, too, is a carrier for the parasite and, above all else, because he has that cassette tape. It is important for the viewer that we explain what it is that Loyen and Tørk need to track down; it's spectacular, a fascinating journey. And right at the end we have put the story of the boy, since Smilla's true aim has been to clear up the matter of his death.

LIKE A SYMPHONY ORCHESTRA

Peter: I certainly did create some problems for Bille and his team, simply because when I wrote *Smilla* I still hadn't learned how to control the entity a novel represents.

I have a friend who compares the writing of a novel to a backpack. For every new chapter you throw in another rock. The problem then becomes that the further you get, the harder and harder it is to lug it around. I prefer to think of the writer as a conductor assembling a symphony orchestra. For every new chapter you send another musician up onto the stage. The beauty of this image is that once you get beyond page 150 you need only give a little flick of a finger to instantly bring on all the basses, all the woodwinds, or the big cymbals. Suddenly, one tiny gesture can refer back to great volumes of text, thus unleashing some very powerful forces in the reader. The drawback comes in the risk of having no special notes to play at the end, even though you are stuck with the task of justifying all your musicians to the reader and yourself, and then seeing them on their way. In this lie the enormous potential and the enormous risks of writing fiction.

With *Smilla*, I do feel that I have, in a sense, passed the buck, having not fully resolved the problem of giving the orchestra something to play. *Borderliners* is the first book in which I have been able to control such an entity from beginning to end. It may be hard for the reader to spot, but it's something which, as a writer, one knows with absolute certainty. For the first time, in *Borderliners*, I found it possible to sustain the state of mind entailed in taking a novel all the way to its conclusion. I wasn't quite capable of that with *Smilla*, but I managed to cover this up by means of various, purely linguistic devices. There are two audio versions of *Smilla*,

New York Times hardcover bestseller list alone. Writing in *The New Yorker*, Fernanda Eberstadt called it "a book of profound intelligence."

In 1993 Peter Høeg published *Borderliners*, and his newest novel, *The Woman and the Ape*, was published in 1996 during the filming of *Smilla*.

a Finnish one and a German, in which I can tell that they have had to contend with things that can basically be put down to what I did not write.

A MATTER OF MENTAL ENERGY

When Thomas Mann was writing a novel he drew on his thousands of index cards and notes. How do you organize your material, Peter? How much of it is a state of mind and how much is technique, when you want the orchestra to strike up?

Peter: The two are inseparable. First and foremost it is a state of mind. A matter of power. Not as when Caruso sings, nor like running a marathon. It's a mental process. A matter, every day for the two years it takes to write a novel, of remaining at one and the same time totally focused and totally relaxed, to save any buildup of tension. To avoid having too many spells when you feel you are the worst writer ever in the history of the world. And so that you can emerge from those swings between megalomania and self-abasement to find a constant pitch and a great delight in your work—something you can sustain. From this, quite of their own accord, spring those sound ideas, the valid conclusions that are, primarily, a state of mind.

The amount of planning involved has varied greatly from book to book. A book such as *Smilla* was very spontaneous and improvised. We had just had a baby and Akinyi, my wife, went back to work soon after the birth, so I just didn't have the energy necessary to research the book thoroughly, I had to fake a lot of things. I was working under much more difficult conditions then than anything I have since been faced with. With *Tales of the Night*, everything was worked out very carefully; that's all part of the classic storytelling tradition. *The Woman and the Ape* is an attempt to hang on to the relaxed feel of *Smilla*, but with a staying power that would obviate any worries about such things as, for example, whether there is anything in reserve for the ending.

THE AUTHOR'S ABILITY TO FORESEE THE FUTURE

The villains' sensational treasure turns out to be a meteorite charged with a form of energy from the birth of the universe, one that might even be alive. A rock that brings to life gruesome parasites which could eradicate all life on earth. As a writer, you seem to have foreseen certain actual events and facts. What did you think when traces of life were suddenly discovered in a meteorite from Mars?

Bille: I felt a surge of relief! I thought to myself, well, now we have some solid proof, now we have something to back up the story. I must remember that when I have to explain the film to the newspaper boys!

Peter: Ha ha. I didn't connect the two things at all. To me the meteorite in *Smilla* is deeply symbolic; I hardly thought of it in concrete terms. I liked the surreal breakdown of realism contained in the book.

When I wrote *Smilla* I had the feeling that no one had ever written anything like it before. Even though I don't keep abreast of things at all, I thought: a woman in this kind of situation, that's new. When I was in New York to meet the press, journalists kept putting book after book in front of me and saying, listen, over here we've got tons of books in which the central characters are women, in unusual and related situations, are you familiar with these? I had never heard of them, but the conclusion I have come to is that no matter how isolated you might feel yourself to be as a writer, you aren't really. We are all connected. As writers, we have taken root in the collective subconscious and hence we cannot help but latch on to things that are common to all people. It's very important that we understand this, not least for the sake of our own humility. We are no more than a tiny ripple on a great river that just keeps on flowing. We are nourished by water that falls on us from above; after a while the ripple disappears, becoming other writers and readers. That's how it always is when you write. You catch hold of something in the collective subconscious that is about to change character. I think that film and literature can act as extremely sensitive seismographs for things that are to follow.

As far as the future of the earth is concerned, I would say that I am becoming less and less pessimistic. If I inquire into my own system, what I find is that those serious crises with which I have been faced in my life—and I've had my share of black days—have nonetheless always led to something positive. The system is purged, and this gives rise to heightened perception and greater sympathy for one's fellow man. That's how it affects me. Deep crises are potentially deeply purifying. The second reason for my feeling less pessimistic is that I have less and less faith in our own ability to control what's going on. To think that we are leading humanity, the earth, toward some kind of total extermination is actually every bit as arrogant as believing that we are capable of founding the millennium. I think there is something that is pushing us from behind, something that is steering us in a particular direction. What that may be, you would have to ask the Dalai Lama, or other people wiser than I. But I have an increasingly clear sense that something—something with purpose or direction—has us in its grip. And I hope that some of this optimism or joy is to be found in my books. Obviously, I'm concerned, too, but since you ask, I have faith in a positive end result.

Bille: I can only go along with Peter. I believe there is a third option.

A Difficult Birth:
The Screenplay

Ann Biderman, scriptwriter

One day a fax came from a friend. It was a brief excerpt from a book called *Smilla's Sense of Snow*. This friend was struck by the beauty of the language and felt that I would love it. I did. Other missives followed over the next few weeks, extraordinary paragraphs about love and loss and exile. Who was this Peter Høeg, and how could I get my hands on a copy of the book?

I first met Bille August sometime in 1992 or early 1993. He admired a script I had written about Georgia O'Keeffe and Alfred Stieglitz. I had seen *The Best Intentions* and *Pelle the Conqueror* and thought he was a wonderful director. He came to Los Angeles and we met.

Then I received a message from my agent, saying that Bille and Bernd Eichinger wished to talk to me about adapting *Smilla*. I was finishing work on a script called *Copycat* and simultaneously doing revisions on *O'Keeffe*. I went to meet them at Bernd's office on Sunset Boulevard. I was deeply engaged in other work and did not know how to solve the problems of adapting this book. On the one hand, it was a poetic interior meditation; on the other, an action thriller climaxing in an ice cave somewhere in Greenland. I did not know how to marry these very disparate elements. I went in, made my pitch, focused on the things that I loved about the book. I did not get the job. I felt a keen sense of loss. I dreamed about Copenhagen and Greenland, Inuits, Smilla.

A while later my agent called and suggested that I write an episode for the TV series *NYPD Blue*. I loved the show and quickly agreed. When I finished the first script, I was offered a staff position. This was sometime in October. I would work on the show until May. I agreed. In April my agent called again. Bille had gotten in a first draft of *Smilla* and they had decided to go with a new writer. Would I be willing to work on it? It was a hard decision. As a screenwriter, I had basically been alone in a room for fifteen years. I now liked being out of my room, liked the deeply collaborative nature of television. At the same time, I missed a deeper connection to my work. David Milch had created this show, these were his characters, it came from his sensibility; I could work in his voice, his idiom, but it would always be *his* voice. I missed my own. It was with great sadness that I left the show, made all the more bittersweet when I won an Emmy Award the following October.

In May, Bille and I flew to Munich to meet with Bernd and start working on *Smilla*. After two days we flew to Copenhagen. Bille took me to all the locations that were in the book. I met some wonderful people and went to the National Museum many times to study the Inuit collections. I saw lice combs, seal-bladder bags, all manner of kayaks and harpoons. I walked the city for days, trying to imagine Smilla and Isaiah and the Mechanic.

I flew back to the States. What had I taken on? I suddenly felt that an attempt to adapt this book was folly of the highest order.

Bille came to Los Angeles, and we got down to work. We made up index cards, one card for each scene, posting them on an enormous bulletin board I had brought over one day. We would have an hour for lunch, take our papers and eat by the pool, surrounded by people yelling into their cellular phones. We talked and talked and talked: What were the themes of the piece? How could we condense the action? Did we or did we not want a voice-over? Could we get away with so many kinds of flashbacks—flashbacks of Smilla and her mother, flashbacks of Smilla and Isaiah, flashbacks of her relationship with the Mechanic? We had many decisions to make. We replaced the worms with nuclear bombs. We made the Mechanic a double agent, felt the love story would not work if he was not on her side.

On and on it went, into June. Bille flew home. I hired a full-time researcher, Joan Cohen, with whom I had worked many times before. For me, one of the great privileges of being a writer is this initiation into another world. I needed to know about the Arctic, about Denmark's relationship with Greenland. I began a serious study of Eskimology, Inuit culture and language. Joan somehow managed to find me an East Greenlandic dictionary. I studied walruses, seal hunting, snow, icebergs, tankers. I knew about ships' engine rooms. My office began to fill up with diagrams of the ship, sent by Bille. Someone would call with bad news and I would think to myself in Inuit *ayornamat*—"it can't be helped." I could tell you how to say "a hill from which one watches the narwhals in the spring." I studied worms and viruses, talked to government agents, listened to the music Smilla had listened to, studied Inuit folktales, string figures, underwater diving operations.

Then I began to write. And I began to understand what had drawn me to this project in the first place. I, too, was a motherless daughter. I did not know where I belonged in the world either. I understood Smilla's rage, her anger and disappointment, her humor. I had experienced the love of a child, romantic confusion, her sense of exile.

In addition to all of this, I was attracted to the mystery/thriller aspects of the piece. There has been foul play. Who killed Isaiah and why? The truth must out. A wrong must be righted. And as in all great works in this genre, in finding out the truth about Isaiah, Smilla finds out the truth about herself.

I was worried about the character of the Mechanic. Something that had been allowed to unfold gracefully over hundreds of pages in the book would have to be abridged. I did not want him, a fully developed character in the book, simply to become an appendage to Smilla in the movie. Peter Høeg had created a sort of role reversal—the Mechanic represents the calm, steady presence while this woman takes action and her life spins out of control. He is the one with the traditional female skills: cooking, keeping a beautiful home. He tends his roses. He embodies a kind of female energy and Smilla a kind of male energy. This was exciting and fun to deal with. I was concerned that the poetic autism he had in the book, evidenced by his dyslexia and stuttering, would not come across on film, and then came to realize that although he had no great verbal acuity, a kind of dignity and gravitas would see him through.

All the characters had phobias and flaws that were great symbolic tools in constructing the piece. Isaiah's deafness was pivotal to the plot, as was Smilla's fear of confinement. The metaphors were wonderful: here was a character who was both spiritually and physically lost at sea.

The first few weeks, months, on a project like this are about a kind of fealty to the novel. You are careful, delicate, you are trying to honor the spirit and tone and intention of the piece. But there also inevitably comes a moment where you must marry your vision to another, you must step away from the orthodoxy of the piece to reach an even truer version of it. It is heretical, you worry, you fantasize about the author and his rage at this betrayal, but there is always that moment where you must make it your own. This is why you were hired to begin with. You dismantle, build, with shabby tools, constantly worried that you are trivializing art.

It took me a year to write the first draft of *Smilla*. Bernd Eichinger was upset, felt that he had missed out on being able to make the film while the book was still an international bestseller. One night I received a fax from Bille telling me that they were going to bring in a new writer, that they loved my script but felt that it needed "a fresh take." Because of the vicissitudes of shooting in extreme weather, there was a specific window of opportunity in which to shoot *Smilla*, and we had missed it. Being replaced as a writer is a common occurrence in Hollywood, but it was still a blow and I felt terrible about it. I also felt that I had taken the time I needed to make the script work. I needed a break from *Smilla*; it had consumed me for a year and a half. Perhaps they were right, and I had gone as far as I could go.

I took a job rewriting a film called *Primal Fear*. I had never doctored a script before, and it was a perfect tonic after the work on *Smilla*. *Smilla* was painstaking, lapidary work. The work on *Primal Fear* was a high-wire act. I was finishing scenes and hand-carrying them to the set, where often they were shot an hour or two later. I sat in on rehearsals, saw how the scenes played, shaped things to the specific needs and talents of the actors.

I stayed on the film until it finished shooting and then spent months in the editing room with the director. In the fall, I took another job, adapting a book that Paramount had bought. I had started working with the author, an ex–New York City detective, when Bille called. They had not liked the draft the new writer had produced and wanted me to come back on the film. I agreed, on two conditions. First, Bille had to come to Los Angeles and focus totally on *Smilla*. I wanted him to articulate exactly what he felt was still needed. If at the end of a week we felt we were in sync, I would proceed with the final draft. In addition, my script would be used as the template for the work we would be doing. Bille agreed; we met and found that we shared similar feelings about what had to be done. Bernd asked Sherry Lansing, the head of Paramount, if they would liberate me for a certain number of weeks, and she generously agreed.

Bille was hard at work on *Smilla*, the giant machinery of a $40 million monster was in motion, and he was being pulled in a thousand different directions at once. We agreed to work for two weeks in New York, the logic being that it was closer than Los Angeles and we would work with less distraction. He would also be able to interview actors during the hours I was writing and did not need him. I would then follow him to Copenhagen.

The work went very well in New York. We started at the beginning of the script, editing, reworking it scene by scene. Bille knew exactly what he wanted, and I was inspired by his energy and commitment. He flew back

Ann Biderman

Ann Biderman has written countless television films and series episodes and has been equally active in work for the big screen. She has been responsible for the screenplays of such box office successes as *Copycat*, starring Holly Hunter and Sigourney Weaver, and Richard Gere's newest film, *Primal Fear*.

Biderman was recently awarded an Emmy for her contribution to the TV series *NYPD Blue*, and she is presently working on, as well as co-producing, a new project based on the life and work of American artist Georgia O'Keeffe.

37

to Copenhagen a few days early; I finished my work and joined him there, new pages in hand. He would read my new work, we would discuss changes, I would revise, and we would move forward. We were organized, marvelously in sync. We did not see daylight for a month. Room service delivered chewing gum and cigarettes on a silver tray. You have no other life, you are cut off from family and friends—a prisoner of the script. Bille had to go to London for casting. I went with him—we were on the final push now, we had a week to go. Bille and I worked feverishly, we were like some cojoined monster, with a common heart . . . we had to finish. He was calm, this calmed me down—we were almost there. Bille gave me some notes on the final scene; I went to type them up and handed them to him an hour before he had to catch his plane. His assistant, Karin Trolle, suggested I make two copies of the floppy disk in case his plane crashed. We went to have a final celebratory lunch, both of us exhausted and very emotional. I thanked him, he thanked me, we embraced, he left with the disk in his pocket—and I have not seen him since.

Greenland: A Brief History

Karin Trolle

The first people are believed to have settled in Greenland about 4,500 years ago. These were the so-called Paleo-Eskimo hunters, who spread from Alaska out over the Arctic and crossed the ice to Greenland at the Kennedy Channel, the "gateway to Greenland." Several migrations ensued, bringing the Independence Cultures, the Saqqaq Cultures, and the Dorset Culture. Because of climatic changes, each wave managed to survive in Greenland for only a certain period of time before dying out, and at times the whole country was completely uninhabited.

The year 1,000 or thereabout saw the arrival of the Thule Culture, that of a hunting people who succeeded in surviving and from whom the contemporary Greenlanders are descended. The Thule Culture was based on the hunting of sea mammals. For transport they used the dog sled, the graceful kayak, and the women's boat. Today the dog sled is still widely used in north and east Greenland, while elsewhere the two boats have been ousted by modern vessels.

Gradually the population spread throughout the country. The Thule Culture declined and is found today in its original form only in the Thule district. To accommodate changing conditions, new techniques for hunting seals and small whales from kayaks were developed, bringing in their wake changes in social structure. This new culture is known as the Inussuk Culture.

Back in 985 Norwegians and Icelanders—the so-called Norsemen— had also begun to settle in Greenland. These were farmers of the Viking culture who supported themselves by working the land in the southwestern part of the country. The Norse population grew to about 4,000, but for some unknown reason—probably connected to the worsening climate—they disappeared from Greenland around 1450.

From 1380 to 1814 the two Kingdoms of Norway and Denmark were ruled by one monarch, with the royal seat in Copenhagen, which explains the historical background of the present union between Denmark and Greenland.

For almost two centuries there were no European settlements in Greenland, but many expeditions and whalers from Europe made for the Greenland waters. Regular contact with Europe was not reestablished until 1721, when, with the help of the Danish king, the Norwegian pastor Hans Egede equipped an expedition to Greenland to convert the Greenland Vikings to Christianity, little knowing that they had vanished long before. A Lutheran mission and trading station was instead established among the Greenlanders around Godthåb Fjord. Thus Greenland became a Danish colony.

In the beginning, the colonization of Greenland was synonymous with an isolationist policy. The Danish authorities feared outside competition and felt that the Greenlandic society was too vulnerable to foreign influences. In 1776 the small trading stations established along the west coast of Greenland consolidated into one company, the Royal Greenland Trade Department, which enjoyed a monopoly until 1950. Progress took its own course as the introduction of trade and the concentration of the population upset the social structure.

The first sign of Greenlandic participation in the decision-making process was seen in 1857 with the establishment of superintendentships having responsibility for some aspects of self-government at a local level. In

1908 two Greenlandic County Councils were established, one in the north and the other in the south. They were later amalgamated to form the Greenland Council.

During World War II, Greenland was cut off from Denmark but received supplies from the U.S.A., and after 1941 the Americans built two military bases in Greenland. (In 1951 they also established the Thule Air

Julia Ormond (Smilla) found the sled dogs' puppies irresistible

Base, still in existence today.) During the war, Greenland's economy was saved by a rare mineral, cryolite, which was essential to the production of aluminum. The cryolite mines are, however, now exhausted and have been closed down.

After the war the country's status seemed somewhat uncertain. The Greenlanders themselves wanted the country to be opened up, and from 1950 efforts were made to create a modern welfare society—heavily supported by Danish subsidies and manpower.

In 1953 Greenland became an integral part of Denmark through an

Ida Julie Andersen (Smilla as a child) and Maliinannguaq Markussen Mølgård (Smilla's mother)

amendment to the Constitution, with two members of the Folketing, the
Danish Parliament. Towns acquired electricity, modern harbors, decent
living accommodations, schools, hospitals, fish factories, and so on. As
time went on, many of the small settlements became depopulated because
of the attraction of the modern towns, especially for the young, and an
ever-increasing number of Danes settled in Greenland. Developments
were governed by Copenhagen, but in the early 1970s the issue of a higher
measure of self-determination arose. In 1972 there was a referendum in
Denmark and Greenland for and against the European Community. More

than 70 percent of the Greenlandic population voted against membership, but nevertheless had to join the community together with Denmark, which voted in favor. The Faeroe Islands, on the other hand, could stay outside the European Community because of their home rule status. This is when the idea of home rule took root in Greenland, and it was established on May 1, 1979.

Today Greenland, like the Faeroe Islands, is an autonomous part of the Kingdom of Denmark.

The Home Rule Act enabled the country to assume responsibility in almost all areas of society. The home rule government consists of the Landsting (the Assembly), the Landsstyre (the Administration), and the civil service.

Between 1979 and 1994 all major areas of administration were handed over to the Greenland home rule government, with the exception of foreign and defense policies, the police, and the administration of justice, which in pursuance of the Home Rule Act are to remain joint affairs of state, formally governed from Denmark.

With the introduction of home rule, Greenland was offered the option of leaving the European Community, an option that was taken up as of February 1, 1985—mainly because of the desire to obtain political control over fishing in Greenland waters. But like a number of other former European colonies, Greenland is affiliated to the community through the so-called OCT arrangement in combination with a special fishing agreement.

The Danish state subsidizes Greenland heavily each year. Initially, the subsidies were intended as development assistance, but today they are considered as more of a regional support scheme.

Sources:
Greenland. The Largest Island in the World. The Arctic Region
of the Danish Realm
Published by the Ministry of Foreign Affairs
Kaalaallit Nunaat Greenland. A Modern Arctic Society
Published by the Greenland Home Rule Government

Theater Director Simon Løvstrøm: Greenlanders in Denmark and Danes in Greenland

Interview with Karin Trolle

Many *Greenlanders regard* Smilla's Sense of Snow *as a Greenlandic novel—it seems almost to have become part of their national heritage.*

Peter Høeg's Smilla is half-Danish, half-Inuit, and Isaiah is Inuit. How do Greenlanders feel about the film being in English, Smilla being played by an Englishwoman, and Isaiah, too, being played by a non-Greenlander?

Well, of course, I've listened to many different Greenlanders airing their views about the film. When we first heard that the novel was to be filmed, there were a lot of us who thought that at long last some of our own, very talented Greenlandic actors were going to have the chance of appearing in a major movie. But later, when we realized that this was going to be a large-scale international production, with an enormous budget, we could well understand that big stars would have to be brought in, to ensure the necessary financial backing. One thing that made it much easier to see the sense in all of this was a visit Bille August made to Nuuk, during which he explained the wider ramifications of the whole affair in a radio interview.

The fact that the boy is not a Greenlander—since he had, after all, to speak English—is not something anyone thinks twice about; he was such a charmer, and so sweet. And as for Julia Ormond, the people of Greenland quite simply took her to their hearts, so receptive was she to Greenlanders and the Greenlandic society, and so interested. She visited a number of local families in their homes.

Everyone is quite convinced that, if nothing else, this film will do a lot to promote a wider knowledge of and a greater interest in Greenland.

The film crew encountered the most amazing goodwill and kindness in Greenland. When one considers what the Danish colonization of Greenland entailed for the Inuit, and the fact that the Danes have not always treated the people of Greenland as well as they might have done, such generosity of spirit came as something of a surprise to me. Is there no bad feeling, no frustration, no downright resentment toward the Danes?

I'm forty now, so I was a child during the fifties and sixties when Greenland was undergoing a process of Danicization. A lot of children, myself included, were packed off to Denmark to learn Danish. Later—in the seventies—Greenlanders became fiercely nationalistic. There are those who might construe this as a hatred of the Danes, but it wasn't that at all. It represented a process through which Greenlanders came to see the importance of preserving their own cultural values and national character in a world that was shrinking by the minute. But we keep very much abreast of international events and we try to teach our children to hold themselves open to the world around them.

As for the hospitality you experienced, that's in the nature of all Greenlanders, and Ilulissat, where the film was shot, is one of the main tourist centers in Greenland.

Your work has brought you into contact with a good many Greenland-

Flashback: The young Smilla and her mother return from a hunting trip and eat raw seal with the other hunters

ers resident in Denmark, although it has to be said mainly with artists, singers, and other individuals who thrive in Danish society. Sadly, however, it is no secret that there are some Greenlanders who never really manage to adjust to Denmark, who "sink to the bottom," turning to alcoholism, drug addiction and petty crime. Have you any idea why they experience such difficulties?

In the fifties a lot of Danish men came to Greenland to work. A good many of them married Inuit women who then accompanied them to Denmark when the time came to go home. I knew of quite a few instances of women who, to begin with, lived what was, relatively speaking, a life of luxury, only, when their children were grown, to find themselves rejected and divorced—as a result of which they have then gone to the dogs.

I have also had friends who moved to Denmark and got into "bad company," started taking drugs, and finally died of overdoses. So the drug scene is partly to blame. There are also a fair number of young Greenlanders who attend further-education courses in Denmark. It may be that some of them have trouble in keeping up with their studies, and if they then happen to bump into a few "kindred spirits" they can easily get caught up in that scene. They just want to give it a try, so off they go to Christiania [a countercultural neighborhood in Copenhagen], experience some sort of "freedom," and it's all downhill from there.

Since the social services setup in Denmark is better than in Greenland there are also a number of unemployed and unemployable who save up for a one-way ticket to Denmark, where they will be financially better off.

But we should never lose sight of the fact that there are ten thousand Greenlanders who, in the name of national unity, have opted to live and make their homes in Denmark; people who are getting on just fine and are fully integrated into Danish society. Of these, perhaps a couple of hundred—concentrated mainly in the Copenhagen area—sink to the bottom, and, unfortunately, it is often these people who stand out most.

How do Greenlanders view the relatively large number of Danes living and working in Greenland? Are they an accepted part of the community, or do they tend to constitute a community within the community?

In Nuuk, the largest town in Greenland, you will find a class structure unheard of anywhere else in Greenland. Nuuk is also the town with the largest number of Danish residents, and here they do indeed constitute a community within the community, endeavoring as they do to maintain the same sort of living standards and contact networks that they had in Denmark. This is not the case in other, smaller, towns and communities. There everyone meets on equal terms. Although, of course, it also depends on the attitude of the individual. Some Danes have actually *chosen* to live in small communities because they feel this offers them a different sort of freedom.

What happens to many Danes *and* Greenlanders who have done a lot of traveling back and forth between the two countries is that after a while in Greenland they start to miss Denmark, and vice versa. I know this from my own experience.

Is there any desire among Greenlanders for a totally independent Greenland, without any sort of political or national link with Denmark?

The political parties in Greenland all have their own views on this point: the Atasut Party would like Greenland to remain part of Denmark, the Siumut Party wants independence once Greenland has reached a stage where it can stand on its own two feet economically, and the Inuit Ataqatiqiit Party has always wanted Greenland to break away completely from Denmark.

In Greenland, as in any other small nation, there is a strong sense of patriotism and national pride, which brings with it a longing for independence. In my younger days I took part in demonstrations for independence myself. But as I grow older I find myself more inclined to face up to reality. After so many years as part of Denmark we have become something of a melting pot, culturally speaking, and we are still financially dependent on Denmark. But the home rule system is a big step in the right direction.

*Simon Løvstrøm is Director of the Silamiut Theater in
Nuuk (Godthåb), Greenland.*

From Copenhagen to Greenland: Filming on Location

Karin Trolle

*S*milla's Sense of Snow was shot in Copenhagen, Ilulissat in Greenland, Kiruna in Sweden, on board the freighter *Kronos* on a variety of more or less ice-covered stretches of sea, and on studio sets in Copenhagen and Munich.

COPENHAGEN

Almost the whole of the first half of the film is set in Copenhagen, and these outdoor scenes, together with a good number of indoor scenes, were shot on location in and around the city.

The fact that Bille August would not be finished mixing another of his films, *Jerusalem*, until February 28, 1996, meant that shooting on *Smilla* could not start until March 4. This was just about as late as we could leave it, since, as we know, this story takes place in winter and we would need snow in all the outdoor shots. All doubts and fears proved groundless, however, when Bille's usual good luck where the weather is concerned also held for this production, manifesting itself in the form of masses of ice and snow and subzero temperatures far into April. As far as the film was concerned, this was just wonderful—a fact that the film crew had to force themselves to bear in mind when Jack Frost was biting hardest and the colds and chest infections set in.

Copenhagen is a beautiful city, offering ample scope for plenty of stunning shots, and Bille August and production designer Anna Asp had no difficulty in coming up with the right settings for *Smilla*. Nor, fortunately, did we encounter any great problem in gaining permission to film wherever we wished, even

(TOP LEFT) *Julia Ormond takes the time to sign autographs for Copenhagen fans.* (TOP RIGHT) *It was necessary to help nature only in a very few scenes. Here the roofs of the White Palace get a little artificial snow.* (LEFT) *On Knippels Bridge in Copenhagen. From the left: Bille August's son Adam, Bille August, director of photography Jörgen Persson, and focus puller Lennart Pettersson*

though the film crew did tend to loom pretty large in the landscape, with all the production vans, umpteen trailers for the cast, a mobile kitchen, a dining room in the shape of an British double-decker bus, and so on and so forth. But the name Bille August acts as a guarantee of earnest endeavor and quality, and that —in conjunction with a star-studded cast—will always open doors.

Among the many Copenhagen locations used was a housing complex on Strand Street that has earned itself the nickname of the White Palace. We had to bother the residents of Strand Street on more than one occasion, disrupting their lives by asking them to hang Christmas decorations in their windows in March, blocking off the street for long spells, and so on. The entries and stairways in the

(TOP) *The view from Smilla's apartment, built in a studio in Copenhagen.* (BOTTOM) *Painter Henrik Axholm next to the model he helped to make*

White Palace were ill suited to our purpose, so all the stairway scenes were shot in buildings in Aldersro Street. Near the start of the film we see Smilla crossing the lovely Knippels Bridge, one of the bridges spanning Copenhagen Harbor, and a car chase was shot one night on Købmager Street and the famous pedestrian street Strøget in the city center, in the presence of a host of extras. Bred Street, too, was pressed into service: the Odd Fellows Mansion doing duty as the exterior of Moritz's club, where Smilla comes to see him during a Christmas party. The actual scene inside the club was, however, filmed at the Hotel d'Angleterre. The scene with Smilla and Isaiah at the National Museum was shot in the Greenlandic section; the autopsy scenes, in the forensic medicine department of Bispebjerg Hospital. Elsa Lübing's apartment is an actual penthouse in the district of Østerbro that boasts a superb view of the city, and the scenes in and around Moritz's house were shot at a house in north Zealand designed by the renowned Danish architect Arne Jacobsen. Last but not least, a fair number of scenes were shot in Copenhagen's North Harbor, also the site of the film's production offices.

Things got particularly hot on the night when the film's special-effects team was scheduled to blow up the ship containing the Arctic Museum. The explosion must have woken up half of Østerbro—but, boy, did it look good! And just as well, since the boat had been bought expressly for that purpose and, for obvious reasons, there was no chance of a retake. The corresponding dramatic scene inside the blazing, sinking ship was shot in a dock at the Institute of Hydraulics, where the special-effects people had constructed a section of the ship interior on a platform that could be rocked back and forth and lowered into the water. Julia Ormond did this scene herself, without a stunt double, so it *is* actually her we see swimming through the hole in the ship's hull! In fact, Julia carried out a number of her own stunts in the film, for which she had prepared with a rigorous physical training schedule involving wall climbing, stunt training, and the like.

The crew was also subjected to a bit of unscheduled drama. The scene that takes place out on the open sea, on the pier connecting the *Kronos* with the oil platform, was shot off Avedøre Holme one exceptionally cold and stormy night. The pier, or actually bridge, had been erected on a number of pontoons, and at one point—before the actors could get out to it, fortunately—the wind was gusting so hard that it set the bridge swaying. This, in turn, caused it to pitch and roll, and a couple of pontoons went down. Even from the shore, with your feet planted solidly on terra firma, it looked danger-

ous; hardly surprising, then, that the set and prop guys, who had worked like fiends out there in the middle of the harbor to save the sinking bridge, appeared somewhat pale and shaken when they finally reached dry land. Luckily, they did manage to save half of the bridge, but the upshot was that we could film in only one direction that night and had to brave the cold again on another night at a later date to shoot the takes from the other direction.

The three apartments in the White Palace—Smilla's, the Mechanic's, and Juliane's—were all constructed at the studio in Tåstrup, to the west of Copenhagen.

(TOP) The producers Martin Moszkowicz and Bernd Eichinger. (BOTTOM) The scenes in Moritz's club were shot at the Hotel d'Angleterre in Copenhagen. Focus puller Lennart Pettersson measures the distance from the camera to Julia Ormond

(TOP LEFT) The scenes in the Arctic Museum that did not require water were shot in a model of the ship built in a studio in Copenhagen. (TOP RIGHT, BOTTOM LEFT AND RIGHT) At the Institute of Hydraulics: because of its complicated construction, the Arctic Museum could tilt and sink

GREENLAND

Some thought had been given to the possibility of shooting the Greenland footage in northern Norway or in Canada, where the infrastructure is more fully developed and where it was felt that production conditions would be more favorable. But in some part of himself Bille August always knew that Greenland was where he would have to go, to find the right mood and the right scenery. As Bille says, "Greenland is the real star of the film. It's a land of majestic character, exerting a strange and powerful influence; and it is this which has made Smilla what she is."

In the town of Ilulissat (or Jakobshavn) on Diskọ Bay about halfway up the west coast of Greenland, Bille found the perfect setting for his film. It was here that the famous polar explorer Knud Rasmussen was born and raised, and it is here, each year, that Greenland's biggest glacier discharges icebergs to the tune of 25 billion tons into the fjord. These stay put, waiting for a high tide when the pressure from within the glacier will push them out beyond the sandbank which has formed at the mouth of the fjord and which the icebergs, because of their vast underwater bulk, cannot negotiate without "help." It is, to say the least, a magnificent and unbelievably beautiful sight to see these ice giants either floating peacefully around in the bay or stuck fast, in winter, when the whole bay is frozen solid.

With a population of 4,600, Ilulissat is the third largest town on Greenland. Its inhabitants earn their living mainly from fishing for

shrimp and halibut, but service industries such as tourism are also important, and it is the hope of many people there that *Smilla*, with its shots of the area, will attract more tourists to Ilulissat.

The last thing August wanted, however, was for the Greenland scenes to have the look of a travelogue or a "Holiday on Ice," since what he was after for the sinister and dramatic scenes enacted here was a bleak, steely-gray atmosphere. It

(TOP) How to make a blizzard: a helicopter rented for the purpose creates wind and stirs up snow. (BOTTOM) The film crew on location in Greenland

55

Bille August gives the last instructions before the ice cave is ready for shooting

tended to be quite sunny around midday while we were on location in Greenland, and so a lot of the takes had to be shot in the morning just around sunrise and in the afternoon around sunset in order to avoid the strongest sunlight.

It goes without saying that filming in Greenland was anything but easy. All the practical details to do with the film crew, transport, catering, hotel accommodations, and so on, were, however, accomplished without a hitch, thanks not least to the invaluable assistance of the local people and the Ilulissat Tourist Bureau. The big problem was the weather, which is constantly changing—and the cold! The technicians were hard put to keep the batteries for the camera and sound equipment warm, and the reels of film were also wrapped in warm blankets to keep the film from cracking in the camera, which can easily happen when working at such low temperatures. On the coldest day of shooting, the temperature dropped to minus 15 degrees F and hot tea and coffee were in great demand!

KIRUNA, SWEDEN

It soon became apparent that the ice cave in which the film's denouement is set could not be built in Greenland, as this called for a very special kind of expertise and very particular types of machinery and equipment. Initially, the idea was to build the ice cave inside a refrigeration plant and, after searching high and low in Denmark with no success, the production department eventually located a plant in Munich big enough to meet our needs. Screeds of drawings and calculations later, however, it turned out that this building's foundations could never take the weight of the volume of ice required for the cave's construction.

Production designer Anna Asp then set off for Jukkas-järvi, near Kiruna in northern Sweden, where she knew of the existence of an ice hotel, built and carved entirely out of ice: the beds, the furniture, the bar, even the drinking glasses. Well-known and highly skilled artists create the most beautiful ice sculptures for it, and there is even an exquisite church. Each year this hotel attracts visitors from every corner of the globe. Guests are furnished with reindeer hides and polar sleeping bags and on waking in the morning are treated to a hot elderberry drink and a sauna (built of wood!).

On board the rusty ship Kronos: *first assistant director Guy Travers confers with Bille August*

When spring comes and the thaw sets in, all this splendor melts away, only to be built again from scratch the following fall.

"Master builders" specializing in ice and snow were of inestimable help when it came to constructing the ice cave. Bulldozers were brought in to build the vast walls, which were then sprayed with water to coat them with ice. Layer upon layer of ice had to be formed, and the surface then textured and painted—a process not without its drawbacks. With the spring sunshine drawing ominously close and the heat from the lamps not exactly doing the ice any good either, the set unit had to work the night shift between takes.

THE *KRONOS*

Finding a ship with a reinforced hull which would be capable of sailing in ice-bound seas but which *on no account* could be red was no easy task. Usually, ships that have to sail in icebound waters are painted red, to make them easier to spot from the air in case they get into difficulties. With the help of a Danish ship broker we did succeed in locating—in Murmansk, of all places—a rather rusty 4,000-ton freighter that had at one time been painted black.

The production company leased this vessel on a time-charter basis; it duly turned up in Copenhagen, complete with Russian crew, and the first week's takes were shot on board, while she was docked in Copenhagen—right outside the windows of the production office in the North Harbor. On board the *Kronos,* we shot scenes on the deck, on the bridge, and in the engine room. The sets for all the other scenes that take place on the ship, in the corridors, cabins, and saloons, were built at a studio in Munich—a large film crew with cameras, lamps, sound equipment, etc., requiring much more space than that afforded by a tiny ship's cabin.

It came as no surprise to anyone that chartering a freighter is an expensive business, but the production department certainly learned a lot about the workings of a port. The *Kronos* had on occasion to be sailed to another part of the harbor, or simply turned around to allow it to be filmed from another angle. This is not something you just do. There are pilotage fees to be paid, and mooring fees, and all sorts of other fees. Nonetheless, it was fun, it was a learning experience, and the Russian crew was extremely helpful and cooperative.

With the takes from the *Kronos* in Copenhagen Harbor and in Avedøre in the can, the ship was dispatched to the frozen waters off the east coast of Sweden, where quite a few shots of the *Kronos* making her way to Greenland through the ice were to be filmed. Chartering the vessel by the day was such an expensive business that we simply had to finish the work on her as quickly as possible, and so a second unit was given the job of filming these scenes while August, the main unit, and the cast carried on shooting in Copenhagen. A second unit is often used for shooting footage that does not involve any actors—street scenes, for example, or car chases and the like, and at one point during the filming of *Smilla,* when the second unit was busy shooting just such footage in Copenhagen, a third unit was sent out into the North Sea with the *Kronos,* to do some helicopter shots of the ship approaching the oil platform.

Englishman Arthur Wooster, the second-unit director, was the man responsible for many of these takes for *Smilla*. A highly experienced director, Wooster is used to filming under extreme conditions, having, among other things, shot all of the second-unit footage for a number of the James Bond films. As Wooster says of the work on board the *Kronos*: "I've been on shoots harder than this, but never colder. It's the first time, for example, I've ever had to be dug out by an ice-breaker before I could get to work . . . I think the most lasting memory I'll take away from this shoot is of the Russian crew. They were wonderful. They're paid very little but never complain, and their ingenuity in making something out of nothing was a humbling experience for us all. For example, their electrical fittings are totally different from ours and I had to ask them for the loan of a plug.

The second-unit crew on the set in Greenland

There was a bit of a wait before they proudly produced one. The next day I asked for another and was told, 'But you've had it.' It turned out it was the only one aboard, and had been taken from the ship's vacuum cleaner."

TRICKS AND DODGES

Often, in making a film, one comes across things which, for whatever reason, cannot be set up or filmed, and so now and again it can be necessary to resort to "tricks and dodges." One of the great aids to modern film production is digital animation, a technique that is becoming more and more widely used in American films. Some films are more or less founded on digital technology: *Death Becomes Her*, *Waterworld*, the *Terminator* films, *Toy Story*, and *Independence Day*, to name but a few. The various techniques involved here are both highly sophisticated and extremely expensive, calling as they do for digital processing of a reel of film frame by frame and in the correct sequence—and we're talking about 25 frames per second.

Here and there in *Smilla's Sense of Snow* it became necessary to resort to digital animation, and a large Los Angeles–based firm, Cinesite, was commissioned to carry out this work. For example, we could hardly arrange to have a meteorite crash-land on Greenland, so this had to be painted onto the film later. Painting things onto a static image is child's play to these amazingly gifted animators. The real difficulties arise when the background and the figures in the frame are in motion, as was the case with the shot in which the Inuit hunter and his dogs are fleeing for their lives from the avalanche triggered by the meteorite's crash landing. For this shot a digital-effects supervisor from Cinesite had to come out to the shoot and set out various markers along the hunter's route—these acting as fixed points, so to speak, to which the animators could refer later on when painting the avalanche, which does eventually engulf the hunter, onto the hundreds of frames in that sequence of film. One advantage of this technique is that it keeps the oncoming avalanche from seeming to jump about in relation to the fleeing hunter. There are all sorts of other rules, too, including how one should shoot vis-à-vis the horizon.

A little help from the digital technicians was also required in another part of the film, namely, the sequence in which Isaiah is seen plunging from the roof. First of all, the film's still photographer Rolf Konow was hoisted high up on a crane to take a picture of the building façade and the street far below: in other words, Isaiah's "route" down from the roof. Then Isaiah was filmed in the act of falling, against what is known as a *green screen*. The terms *blue screen* or *green screen* refer to the technique of painting a backdrop in a special blue or green color which, to put it in layman's terms, can be easily overlaid, on the computer, with another filmed or photographed background. To produce the actual falling action, the film's special-effects team built a weird and wonderful contraption: a long pole that could be moved up and down. Clipper Miano, who plays Isaiah, was strapped to the top of this pole and then filmed from high up on a gantry while the apparatus traveled downward, spinning slightly on its own axis. But the terrified expression on the boy's face looks to have been pretty spontaneous! It has to be said, though, that the safety levels on film sets are very high indeed, especially, as one might expect, where children are involved, and at no point was Clipper in any danger. His dad, who was there at the time, can vouch for that!

Clipper Miano (Isaiah) is filmed while he floats downward attached to a strange contraption. Later, this piece of film will be digitally transferred to the correct background

Interview with Producer Bernd Eichinger

Interview with Karin Trolle

Y*ou trained as a film editor—and worked as such. You have also directed movies. What made you want to become a producer?*

I attended film school in West Germany in the early seventies. At that time there was no film industry to speak of in Germany and the only directing work to be had was in television. I didn't find that challenging enough and decided to switch to producing. I had written a lot of scripts, so now I started producing my own work. Between 1973 and 1979 I was involved in the production of fifteen movies—mostly films financed by television. But the first "real" movie I produced independently was *Christiane F.*

In 1979 I got the chance to buy into the German distribution company Constantin Film GmbH.

I was constantly shuttling back and forth between Hollywood and Germany in order to buy films for distribution in Germany, but it was only in 1982, when I produced *The Neverending Story,* that I really formed close links with Hollywood. I realized that I had to have a company in Hollywood, since that's where the writers, the actors, the agents, and the studios are. So in 1990 I opened an office there, Constantin Film Development, which develops new projects.

As a producer, once you have found a movie project you want to make, how do you normally go about it getting it financed? Where do you start?

Well, there are probably a million ways to go about it, but I can tell you how I do it. We have people working day and night to find good projects.

Once we have found a story we want to make, we have to find a good screenwriter and develop the screenplay. When the screenplay begins to take shape we start looking for a director. Then we start casting.

Once we have a finished screenplay, a director, and a cast, we go out on the world market to find a good distribution network. This so-called presale is part of the financing, and my idea is that it should cover 60 to 70 percent of the budget. At Constantin Film we have a very good banking arrangement to finance the last part.

Bille August and producer Bernd Eichinger

I have a feeling that in America the agents are in a much more powerful position than in Europe—in Scandinavia most actors don't even have agents. How does the American agent system work?

The agent system has its advantages and its disadvantages. The agents know everything that goes on and it's their job to bring people together, something that is often a great help. But sometimes it's as if they're trying to keep people apart. For example, sometimes an actor wants to play a part in a project he or she likes and is willing to compromise on the normal salary if it's beyond the producer's budget. Agents hate that because they are paid 10 percent of the salary, so they really try to avoid that kind of situation. Actors' agents often have an idea of how the career of their clients should be and do not want them playing characters that deviate too far from this.

Writers' agents can be very useful, inasmuch as they give you hints of new projects coming up. But sometimes they want to sell you everything, because

Bernd Eichinger

After studying at the Munich Film and Television School, Bernd Eichinger worked in many branches of the industry before turning to writing and directing his own scripts. In 1974 he formed Solaris Film Production, which in its first five years produced films by such eminent German directors as Wim Wenders, Wolfgang Petersen, Alexander Kluge, Hans Jürgen Syberberg, and Edgar Reitz.

In 1979 Eichinger took over Neue Constantin Film, and its reputation was established almost immediately with the success of Wolfgang Petersen's *The Neverending Story,* followed by Jean-Jacques Annaud's production of *The Name of the Rose,* starring Sean Connery; a new adaptation of Hubert Selby's *Last Exit to Brooklyn; Salt on Our Skin,* starring Greta Scacchi; and *The Cement Garden* by Andrew Birkin.

Eichinger's association with Bille August began with *The House of the Spirits.* More recent films include Sonke Wortmann's *Der Bewegte Mann.*

The above films have won Eichinger a great number of German and international film awards, among them Bavarian Film Awards, Golden Screen Awards, a César Award, and a

they have so many scripts on their desks.

Then there are the lawyers and the business managers. Sometimes they are really crazy, and with all these people intervening, the work of coordinating things is made more and more complicated.

When you have to deal with the actors' agents it is important that you have a good script with good parts for the actors *and* a good director. Then you're off to a good start. In the case of both *The House of the Spirits* and *Smilla's Sense of Snow* we had good scripts and we had Bille. In this game, the director's the key factor.

Once the film is made, you then want to sell it to those territories to which it has not already been presold. What's the best way to go about this?

My theory is that if you haven't been able to sell the film in advance, then there is something wrong with the concept and in that case it's going to be very hard to sell the film later on.

You work in both Germany and the United States. I suppose ways of working differ to some extent in these two countries. Which of the two do you prefer to work in, and has your not being an American ever been a handicap to you as a producer in Hollywood?

I make films in Germany mainly for the German market. Because of the limited amount of money in the German film business, these tend to be low-budget films featuring German actors. And I make very expensive English-language films with British and American stars destined for an international market.

The main reason why things are much easier for me in Germany is that I am the biggest film producer there, and so everybody wants to work with me. In Hollywood, film projects pile up on the producers' desks, among them ideas for quite a few major movies. There are only so many writers, directors, and stars, so the competition is tough. The process of developing a project is very complex and exhaustive. But I have never seen it as a handicap that I am not American.

What was it in Smilla's Sense of Snow *that made you want to produce this movie? What was it in the story that you liked and that made you believe in it as a film?*

Having finished the shooting of *The House of the Spirits* I was looking for good material because I wanted to make another movie with Bille. Then Bille sent me Peter Høeg's novel *Smilla's Sense of Snow* and asked me to read it. I liked it a lot and thought it contained a number of most intriguing elements.

First of all, Smilla. She is a very strong female heroine and a very interesting character. On the one hand she is a wild kid from Greenland who is most at ease when she is away from the civilized world. On the other hand she is a scientist with a very scientific and logical working mind.

The setup is also fascinating: a film shot entirely in winter and some of it shot at the end of the world. And the thriller aspect is excellent, and rather unusual.

But keeping all these elements in the script was difficult. It was a very difficult process—it took two years and three writers.

How did your collaboration with Bille start? Do you recall your first meeting?

I had read the novel *The House of the Spirits* and was eager to make it into a film, but I knew that Warner had the rights. A couple of years later, when nothing had happened, I made inquiries, and here the agents' network proved helpful, because very soon a lawyer called me to confirm I was interested, after which he sent me the script. It was not perfect, but it was very good, so off I went to Stockholm, where Bille was then working on *The Best Intentions*. We had a meeting, we hit it off, and I decided to buy the rights from Warner, who for various reasons was willing to sell.

That is how my very happy collaboration with Bille began, and I hope that we will make many more movies together after *Smilla's Sense of Snow*.

Silver Bear.

Although Eichinger is first and foremost a producer, he continues to write scripts and to direct films from time to time. In 1996 he wrote and directed a television film, *Das Mädchen Rosemarie (The Girl Rosemary)*.

The Ice Cave, the *Kronos*, and the White Palace: Setting the Scene for *Smilla*

Anna Asp, Production Designer

*T*he three largest sets in Smilla's Sense of Snow *are of the apartments in the White Palace, all of which were constructed at the studio in Copenhagen, the interior of the freighter* Kronos, *which was built on Bavaria Film's studio sound stages in Munich, and the ice cave, which really was built out of ice in the small town of Jukkasjärvi near Kiruna in Lapland, in the north of Sweden. Bavaria Film's studios were chosen as the location for the filming of the interior shots of the* Kronos *because the company mainly responsible for producing the film, Constantin Film, is based in Munich, and the studios there were big enough to accommodate the erection of such a set. The choice of Jukkasjärvi as the site for the ice cave was prompted by the fact that this is one place where they have plenty of experience in building with ice and snow. Every year an ice hotel, consisting of a series of interconnecting igloos, is constructed in this little town.*

Here is how the Oscar-winning production designer Anna Asp went about designing and building these three sets.

THE THREE APARTMENTS: SMILLA'S, THE MECHANIC'S, AND JULIANE'S

Since these three apartments are set one above the other in the same building, they all have the same layout. But obviously each one had to be decorated quite differently to fit the three characters living in them. These apartments had to reflect the personalities of Smilla, the Mechanic, and Juliane.

Juliane recalls Greenland in the bright colors of childhood, with folk art, snowflakes painted on the floor and furniture, hand-cured hides and woven rugs on the walls. And, of course, an awful mess—indicative of the way in which her life is falling apart.

Smilla's apartment is the absolute antithesis of this, showing how two people with a common past may differ greatly in their recollection of it. Smilla's decor is minimalist, almost monochrome. Dark-colored floors reflected in glass give an illusion of mountains, ice, and wide-open spaces.

The Mechanic has feminine cooking and decorating skills, so his apartment is tastefully furnished with cushions and plants and a wonderful kitchen. To keep the masculine touch, the colors are mainly brown.

THE *KRONOS*

Bille August wanted a black ship, to give an impression of mystery and danger. And since

we would be having it sail through ice-covered waters, this vessel needed to have a reinforced hull. Eventually we did succeed in locating a black—and extremely rusty—Russian ship, in Murmansk. Having seen the "style" of the ship and its external aspect, I was then in a position to start work on the interior. I have tried to make it seem as claustrophobic as possible, in order to convey the appropriate, sinister atmosphere—submarine-like, almost. I had photographed all the ships we

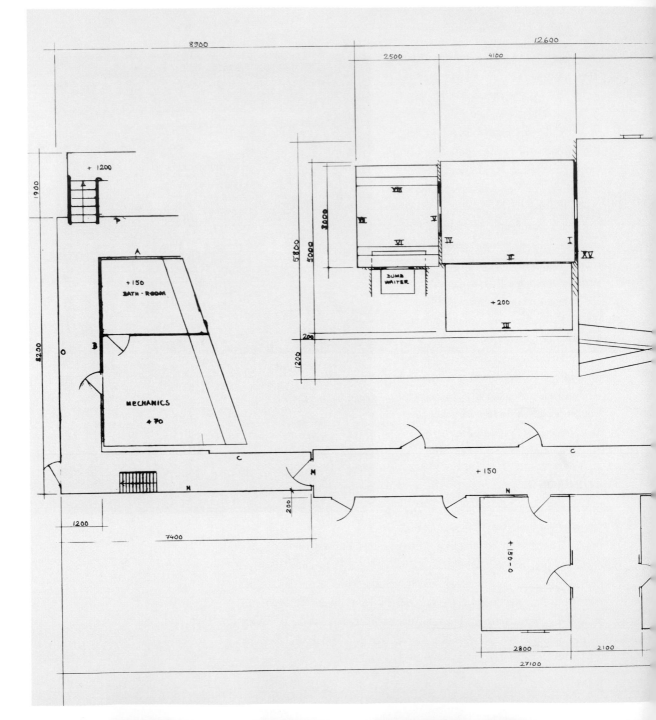

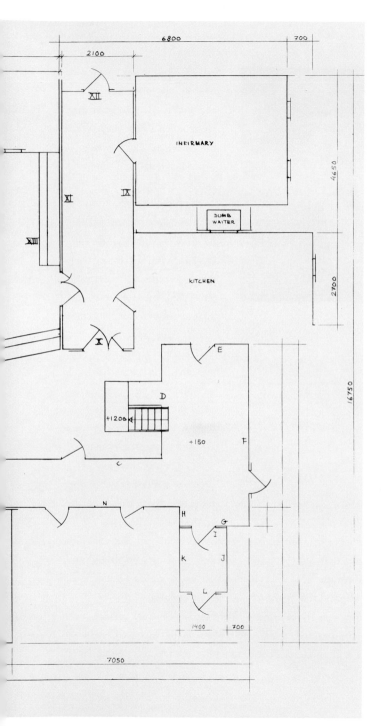

Anna Asp wished to create a claustro-phobic atmosphere in the labyrinthine corridors of the Kronos. *Drawing by the Swedish draftsman and carpenter Love Malmsten*

had gone over in our hunt for the right *Kronos* from every conceivable angle, and in designing the sets I have made use of everything from these that I felt a woman would find brutal and dangerous and frightening.

Almost all the lighting on board the ship is an integral part of the set design, and, in order to emphasize Smilla's terror during the chase scenes, lights were also inset low down on the walls and on the floor, to throw menacing shadows upward.

The colors on board the ship were chosen in shades that would accentuate the faces of the actors to the full, but without dominating them. While the color scheme also serves to create an atmosphere, I wanted the shots to contain a degree of contrast, which is why the color scheme tends to border on the black/white scale.

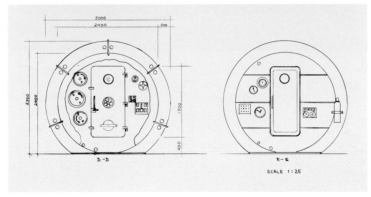

(TOP) *Cargo hold one.* (BOTTOM) *The door between cargo holds one and two. Drawing by Love Malmsten*

The corridor with all the cabins opening off it was built in the shape of a large U, to enable the actors to disappear up a stairway or around a corner, only to pop up again somewhere else. This makes it impossible for the audience to find its bearings on the ship and adds to the feeling of claustrophobia.

The cargo holds were also constructed in the studio. The walls and floors are supposed to be of rusting iron, and the metal plates on the floors are all numbered—an idea I got from seeing photographs of a nuclear power station. This is where the scientists keep all their equipment and the apparatus to be used on the expedition, and the problem here was that while all this equipment obviously had to be stowed away and lashed down, the interior also had to seem impressive, ultramodern, and scientifically intriguing. We solved this problem by wrapping everything in plastic, from the helicopter right down to the smallest aluminum box. And then we tied the whole lot down with very coarse rope.

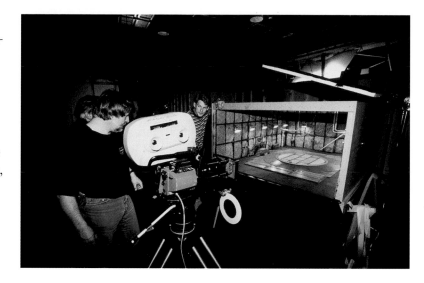

Camera operator Jamie Harcourt with the camera in front of the model of cargo hold two

The number one hold opens onto the number two hold, which the scientists have fitted out for the storage of the large and mysterious "treasure" they are sailing to Greenland to find and bring back to Denmark. Inspiration for the number two hold was drawn entirely from nuclear power stations. The actors never set foot inside number two hold; they only peer in at it through a window in the door, so this room was built as a 1:10 scale model.

THE ICE CAVE, THE LAKE, AND THE METEORITE

I think the toughest assignment on this film was the construction of the ice cave. Originally, we had planned to build this in a refrigeration plant in Munich, but then we found that no foundation would ever be able to cope with the volume of ice required, and in the end we decided to build it on an outdoor site in northern Sweden. I got in touch with Jukkasjärvi Ltd, the people who build the ice hotel up there each year. They took on the job of building the cave walls out of snow, after which two artists, Arne Bergh and Åke Larsson, carved ice formations out of the

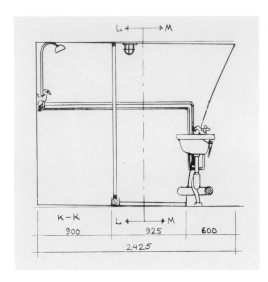

K–K
900

L ← → M
925

600

2425

(ABOVE) *The shower in the Mechanic's cabin on board the* Kronos. *Drawing by Love Malmsten.* (RIGHT) *The crew working on the ice cave*

six-foot-thick, twenty-seven-foot-high walls. For this they used all sorts of tools, from huge pieces of digging equipment to fine, custom-made hand tools from Japan.

By the time the walls had acquired the sculptural form we were looking for, the days were getting longer and warming up a little. So when we got to the point of covering the walls with a 1/10-inch-thick layer of ice, we had to work in shifts night after night, using a garden hose with a very fine nozzle to spray the cave walls with water, to ensure that the water would freeze solid the moment it hit the wall. The temperature in there could not rise above 20 degrees F during the day, and it was very cold at night, dropping a low as minus 5 degrees F. The same was true when it came to painting the ice-covered walls. The paint was sprayed on with the help of a large compressor, with a dash of pure alcohol added to the paint to stop the valve on the nozzle from freezing up. The painter sprayed the walls from a cage mounted on a truck. It was vital that the paint should freeze

Storyboard artist Carl Aldana's first drawing of the ice cave, with the meteorite in the middle of the lake

as soon as it came in contact with the icy surface, otherwise it would run. We were treading a very fine line at all times.

All these difficulties notwithstanding, we did succeed in having the 165-foot-long and 65-foot-wide ice cave ready by the time the film crew arrived. The only problem was that the spring sunshine showed up along with them, causing the paint to melt from the walls. We were left with walls of a lighter color than I had envisaged and, as it was, I had not dared use too strong a blue for the walls, for fear that the set would end up looking like an advertisement for menthol cough drops. After all, the cave was meant to form the setting for a scientific expedition and an extremely dangerous situation for Smilla.

The ice cave was built with the idea that all the scientists would be wearing helmets fitted with safety lamps, and that they would be carrying torches. We also had floodlights on view in the shots, and here, too, I wanted to have the light shining upward, casting oversized shadows onto the walls to give some impression of the vast scale of the ice cave.

Anna Asp

Anna Asp was born in Sweden and is a graduate of the Swedish Academy of Fine Arts and the Royal Swedish Institute of Drama.

Asp was responsible for the production design on many of Ingmar Bergman's later films, among them *Autumn Sonata, Face to Face,* and *After the Rehearsal,* as well as *Fanny and Alexander,* for which she won an Academy Award.

Asp's long list of credits also includes such films as Roy Andersson's *Giliap* and Andrei Tarkovsky's last film, *The Sacrifice.*

Asp designed the sets for Bille August's most recent films: *Pelle the Conqueror, The Best Intentions, The House of the Spirits,* and *Jerusalem.*

Crew Biographies

Jörgen Persson—Director of Photography

Jörgen Persson was born in Sweden in 1946. He has photographed a great number of Swedish movies and is especially known for his long collaboration with Bo Widerberg on many of his films, among them *Elvira Madigan*, *Ådalen '31*, and *Joe Hill*.

Persson has also worked with other eminent Scandinavian directors; his films include Lasse Hallström's *The Cock* and *My Life as a Dog*, Hans Alfredson's *The Singleminded Murderer*, and Liv Ullman's *Sophie*.

Persson first worked for Bille August on *Pelle the Conqueror* and has filmed all his movies since then: *The Best Intentions*, *The House of the Spirits*, and *Jerusalem*.

Janus Billeskov Jansen—Editor

Janus Billeskov Jansen was born in Denmark in 1951. He entered the Danish film industry in 1970 and has since then edited almost thirty feature films, including the Danish director Nils Malmros's *Boys* and *The Tree of Knowledge*, Søren Kragh Jacobsen's *Thunderbirds*, and Max von Sydow's *Katinka*.

Jansen has edited the entire Bille August repertory: *In My Life*, *Zappa*, *Twist and Shout*, *Pelle the Conqueror*, *The Best Intentions*, an episode of *The Indiana Jones Chronicles*, *The House of the Spirits*, and, most recently, *Jerusalem*.

For both *Pelle the Conqueror* and *The House of the Spirits* Jansen was awarded the Danish Film Academy Award for best editing.

Barbara Baum—Costume Designer

Barbara Baum lives in Berlin and has worked with many eminent film directors. From 1972 until his death in 1982, she worked almost exclusively with Rainer Werner Fassbinder, designing the costumes for such films as *Effie Briest*, *The Marriage of Maria Braun*, *Berlin Alexanderplatz*, *Lili Marleen*, *The Longing of Veronika Voss*, and *Querelle*.

Baum's more recent films include *Burning Secret* by Andrew Birkin, *Voyager* by Volker Schlöndorff, B*ecoming Colette* by Danny Huston, *The House of the Spirits* by Bille August, and TV miniseries such as *Fathers and Sons* by Bernhard Sinkel and *The Life of Hemingway* and *Catherine the Great* by Marvin J. Chomsky.

Among the actors for whom Baum has designed costumes in all these movies are Hanna Schygulla, Barbara Sukowa, Armin Müller-Stahl, Rosel Zech, Jeanne Moreau, Brad Davis, Faye Dunaway, Klaus Maria Brandauer, Sam Shepard, Julie Delpy, Mathilda May, Meryl Streep, Glenn Close, Jeremy Irons, Winona Ryder, Antonio Banderas, and Vanessa Redgrave.

Baum received the Venice Film Festival Award for Best Costume Design in 1988 for *Burning Secret* and the Bavarian Film Award in 1993 for her work on *The House of the Spirits*.

Hans Zimmer—Composer

German composer Hans Zimmer has for many years been working in Hollywood, where he has his studio. He has written the music for a great number of major movies, among them: *Black Rain* and *Thelma and Louise* by Ridley Scott, *A World Apart* by Chris Menges, *Rain Man* by Bernard Rose, *Driving Miss Daisy* by Bruce Beresford, *Green Card* by Peter Weir, *Regarding Henry* by Mike Nichols, *Toys* by Barry Levinson,

Renaissance Man and *A League of Their Own* by Penny Marshall, *The House of the Spirits* by Bille August, *The Lion King* by Rojer Allers and Rob Minkoff, *Crimson Tide* by Tony Scott, *Nine Months* by Chris Columbus, and *Broken Arrow* by John Woo.

Zimmer was nominated for an Academy Award for *Rain Man* in 1988 and for a Grammy Award for *Driving Miss Daisy*. He won both the Academy Award, the Golden Globe Award, and the Grammy Award for *The Lion King* in 1994, and a Grammy Award in 1995 for *Crimson Tide*.

Chris Munro—Production Sound Supervisor

British sound engineer Chris Munro started work as trainee sound maintenance engineer at Elstree Studios in 1968, leaving in the early seventies to work freelance on *The Persuaders* TV series with Tony Curtis and Roger Moore. He also worked as a freelance sound maintenance engineer and boom operator on numerous feature films, television and commercials until 1975, when he was offered the chance to mix second unit on *Cross of Iron* for Sam Peckinpah.

Munro has more than twenty years' experience as a production mixer. His work includes *A Prayer for the Dying* by Mike Hodges, *Backbeat* by Ian Softley, *A Business Affair* by Charlotte Brandstrom, *Robin Hood: Prince of Thieves* by Kevin Reynolds, *The Russia House* by Fred Schepisi, *A Fish Called Wanda* by Charles Crichton, *Judge Dredd* by Danny Cannon, *Fierce Creatures* by Robert Young, and *A Midsummer Night's Dream* by Adrian Noble.

Munro is a director and active partner in Twickenham Sound Station Ltd, a company specializing in digital audio postproduction, which has done the digital processing for such feature films as *The Crucible*, *Interview with the Vampire*, *Nell*, *Little Buddha*, *Backbeat*, and *Damage*.

Part Two

JULIA ORMOND

GABRIEL BYRNE   RICHARD HARRIS

SMILLA'S SENSE OF SNOW

A BERND EICHINGER PRODUCTION
A BILLE AUGUST FILM

CONSTANTIN FILM PRESENTS
A BERND EICHINGER PRODUCTION   A BILLE AUGUST FILM
JULIA ORMOND   GABRIEL BYRNE   RICHARD HARRIS   *SMILLA'S SENSE OF SNOW*
ROBERT LOGGIA   JIM BROADBENT   MARIO ADORF   BOB PECK   TOM WILKINSON
EMMA CROFT   PETER CAPALDI   JÜRGEN VOGEL   and VANESSA REDGRAVE
Casting by LEONORA DAVIS   Production Executive DIETER MEYER
Second-Unit Director ARTHUR WOOSTER   Director of Photography JÖRGEN PERSSON
Production Designer ANNA ASP   Costume Designer BARBARA BAUM
Edited by JANUS BILLESKOV-JANSEN   Music by HARRY GREGSON-WILLIAMS and
HANS ZIMMER   Screenplay by ANN BIDERMAN   Based upon the novel by
PETER HØEG *Frøken Smillas fornemmelse for sne*
(originally published by Munksgaard/Rosinante Publishers)
Produced by BERND EICHINGER and MARTIN MOSZKOWICZ
Directed by BILLE AUGUST

A German-Danish-Swedish coproduction Constantin Film Produktion GmbH in
cooperation with Smilla Film A/S, Greenland Film Production AB, and Bavaria Film GmbH.
This film was supported by EURIMAGES, FFA, Film FernsehFonds Bayern, the
Danish Film Institute, Hans Hansen, and the Nordic Film- & TV Fund

Dolby Digital   Constantin Film   Summit

THE CAST

Smilla JULIA ORMOND
The Mechanic
GABRIEL BYRNE
Tørk RICHARD HARRIS
Moritz ROBERT LOGGIA
Lagermann
JIM BROADBENT
Lukas MARIO ADORF
Loyen TOM WILKINSON
Ravn BOB PECK
Jakkelsen JÜRGEN VOGEL
Lander PETER CAPALDI
Benja EMMA CROFT
Elsa Lübing
VANESSA REDGRAVE
Juliane AGGA OLSEN
Isaiah CLIPPER MIANO
Telling DAVID HAYMAN
Licht ALVIN ING
Verlaine LARS BRYGMANN
Detective
MATTHEW MARSH
Hansen ERIK HOLMEY
Maurice PETER GANTZLER
Policeman PATRICK FIELD
Mrs. Lagermann
CHARLOTTE BRADLEY
Mrs. Schou
ANN QUEENSBERRY
Pastor CHARLES LEWSEN
Smilla as a Child
IDA JULIE ANDERSEN
Smilla's Mother
MALIINANNGUAQ
MARKUSSEN MØLGÅRD
Inuit Hunter
ONO FLEISCHER

THE CREW

Director BILLE AUGUST
Producers
BERND EICHINGER and
MARTIN MOSZKOWICZ

Screenplay by
ANN BIDERMAN
Based upon the Novel by
PETER HØEG
Music by HANS ZIMMER
and HARRY GREGSON-
WILLIAMS
Editor
JANUS BILLESKOV-JANSEN
Director of Photography
JÖRGEN PERSSON
Production Designer
ANNA ASP
Costume Designer
BARBARA BAUM
Second Unit Director
ARTHUR WOOSTER
Casting by LEONORA DAVIS
*Executive in Charge of
Production* DIETER MEYER

Associate Producer
ROSANNE KORENBERG
Production Supervisor
THOMAS HEINESEN
Production Manager
MARIANNE CHRISTENSEN
1st Assistant Director
GUY TRAVERS
2nd Assistant Director
EMMA POUNDS
3rd Assistant Director
WILLIAM BOOKER
Dialogue Coach
PENNY DYER
Continuity
ANNEMARIE AAES
Production Coordinators
ILSE SCHWARZWALD,
MARIANNE JUL HANSEN
Production Assistants
NANNA
MAILAND-HANSEN,
LOUISE BIRK PETERSEN
Production Assistant, Munich
OLAF SCHMIDT
Production Assistant, Sweden
MARITA KOIVISTO
Office Receptionist
ANJA CHRISTENSEN

Location Manager, Denmark
MOUNS OVERGAARD
Location Assistants, Denmark
KASPER BARFOED,
ANDREAS FUGL
THØGERSEN
Location Scouts
HANS PLOUGH,
LARS VALENTIN, NICO
*Location Consultant,
Greenland*
STRANGE FILSKOV
Location Consultants, Sweden
EVA LUNDQVIST,
YNGVE BERGQVIST
Assistant to Mr. August
KARIN TROLLE
Assistants to Mr. Eichinger
BOBBY DELORA,
NICOLE SILVERTON
Assistants to Mr. Moszkowicz
BETTINA ZSCHORNACK,
NATHANIEL WALTERS,
CHRISTA DIEBITZ
Assistant to Ms. Korenberg
MELISSA BABYAK
Assistant to Julia Ormond
BRIAN PINES
Assistant to Gabriel Byrne
GEMMA MASSOT
Assistant to Richard Harris
EVA JUEL
Trainer to Julia Ormond
RICHARD SMEDLEY
Chaperones for Clipper Miano
PASCAL MIANO,
ULRIK BIRK PETERSEN
London Consultant
STUART LYONS
Casting Director, Munich
RISA KES
Casting Director, Copenhagen
TOVE BERG BRAMSEN
Extras Casting, Greenland
SIMON LØVSTRØM
Still Photographers
ROLF KONOW,
OLE KRAGH-JACOBSEN
Camera Operator
JAMIE HARCOURT

Focus Puller
LENNART PETTERSSON
Steadycam Operator
MIKE TIVERIOS
Clapper/Loaders
JAN PALLESEN,
DANIEL PARMO
Key Grip GARY
HUTCHINGS
Grip JONATHAN TOWLER
Grip, Germany
ROLAND BERGER
Grip Truck Driver
TORBEN FRANK
Production Sound Supervisor
CHRIS MUNRO
Boom Operator
COLIN WOOD
Sound Assistants
CLAUS LYNGE,
JONAS LANGKILDE
Sound Assistant, Germany
PETER BRÜCKLMAIR
Gaffer
SØREN LYS SØRENSEN
Best Boy THOMAS NEIVELT
Pre-rigging Gaffer
BERNIE GRILL
Pre-rigging Best Boy
LUDWIG BRUNNHOFER
Electricians MOGENS OTTE,
TORBEN BORUP-MADSEN,
THOMAS LARSEN,
NIELS RASK
Electricians, Germany
WOLFGANG KRAUTTER,
JANIS NESPETHAL
Stunt Coordinator
PAUL WESTON
Stunt Doubles
SY HOLLANDS,
DEL BAKER, GABE
CRONNOLLY, DAVID
FORMAN, DENI JORDAN,
BO THOMAS
Safety Divers
CLAUS GOTFREDSEN,
PETER BUHL
Stand-ins for Julia Ormond
KIM SAMSON,
JEANETTE MADSEN

Stand-in Utility THOMAS WILLIAM RASMUSSEN

Special FX Supervisor PETER HUTCHINSON

Special FX Coordinator BRENDA HUTCHINSON

Senior Special FX Technicians DAVID BRIGHTON, DAVID ELTHAM

Special FX Technicians RICHARD BROWN, STEPHEN HUTCHINSON, JIM CROCKETT, HUMMER HØIMARK, PETER HØIMARK, HANS PETER LUDVIGSEN, ALLAN ELKJÆR, ANDREAS BALSLEV-OLESEN, JESPER DAMGAARD SØRENSEN, LARS KOLDING ANDERSEN

Costume Designer for Julia Ormond MARIT ALLEN

Assistant to Barbara Baum TIM ASL.\M

Wardrobe Supervisor MARCO SCOTTI

Dresser for Julia Ormand GEORGINA GUNNER

Dresser, Denmark and Greenland OLE KOFOED

Dresser JANE BARLEBO ANDERSEN

Assistant Dresser EVA SVENNINGSEN

Seamstress ELSE PRANGSGAARD

Makeup and Hair Supervisors GERLINDE KUNZ, HORST STADLINGER

Makeup and Hair Assistants PER CHRISTENSEN, MALIN BIRCH-JENSEN

Production Accountant KLAUS HOLZNER

Assistant Accountant MARIA WURLITZER

Accountants, Denmark CHARLOTTE MORTENSEN, HENRIK SCHÆBEL, ADA KAALUND

Cashier DITTE CHRISTIANSEN

Assistants to Production Designer ANN-MARGRET FYREGÅRD, ANNELIE WEMSTAD

Art Director, Munich JÜRGEN STRASSER

Assistant Art Director PAVEL PITTNER

Set Decorator IVAR BAUNGAARD

Assistant Set Decorator LEIF THINGTVED

Set Decorator, Sweden CECILIA SILLE HERSBY

Property Master PETER GRANT

Property Master, Munich ANDREAS REIF

Prop Woman SIMONE GRAU LARSEN

Prop Assistant CHRISTIAN ZETHNER

Prop Drivers CLAUS PITZNER, JAN LENNART DE LA PORTE

Storyboard Artist SIMON BANG

Ice Sculptors ARNE BERGH, ÅKE LARSSON

Construction Manager ANDERS ENGELBRECHT

Carpenters OLE LOCHMANN, KLAUS MALMGREN, FRANZ TRNKA, JAC OLSEN, JAN PALLAVICINI, NICOLAI PAULSEN, FLEMMING PLEH, MATTI MALKAMAA

Carpenter/Drawings LOVE MALMSTEN

Painters KRISTOFER SJÖSTRÖM, PER JOHANSSON, BIRGITTE THIESEN ROSENSTAND, HANS ERIK OLSEN

Standby Painter HENRIK AXHOLM

Chauffeurs THOMAS CARLSON, JOSEPH KASPAR, TONY CASTLE, ULRICH MAY, PETER ANDRESEN, JENS UBERT, BETTINA GÖRGNER, MOLLY PLANK

Set Runner, Denmark KAARE SEIFERT BOESKOV

Production Runners, Denmark CHRISTIAN CHRISTIANSEN, NICOLAI WILLADSEN, JESPER GRAND, NIKOLAJ KOFOED

Drivers, Denmark EVALD ROOS, SØREN OTTOSEN, NANNA SYLVEST VIERØ

Minibus Drivers, Denmark ANDERS W. LUND, MARTIN STRANGE-HANSEN

Drivers, Germany RAINER LHOTZKY, HELEN PIRPAMER

Minibus Drivers, Germany WOLFGANG EXEL, DOMINIK WEISSER

Facility Drivers, Denmark WILLIES WHEELS: GARY FIDLER, BRYAN BAVERSTOCK, KIM WORLEY, PATRICIA O'CONNELL, JOHN TOPPING

Drivers, Sweden LEIF BRAND, PATRICK SAHLÉN, PETTER RANESTÅHL, KENT STURK, JOAKIM LUNDSTRÖM, BOSSE JOHANSSON

Catering, Denmark KOKKERIET

Catering, Greenland KENNETH SANDER

Catering, Germany KARIN KUGLER

Housekeeper for Julia Ormond KERSTI NÄSLUND

Supercargo ERIK SJØLIN

Ship Broker MOGENS SØRENSEN

Ice Consultant PALLE ERIKSEN

Standby Medicals JØRGEN WORM, KATHRINE KAARIS

Nurse KIM KJÆRULFF

Veterinarians JENS MØLLER, STIG TABER

Dog Handler CARSTEN CARNETT

International Publicity GINGER CORBETT, CHARLOTTE TUDOR

Unit Publicist, Germany SILKE FUHRMANN

Unit Publicist, Scandinavia CHRISTEL HAMMER

Second Unit

1st Assistant Director TERRY MADDEN

Production Manager STEFAN ZÜRCHER

Camera Operator TIM WOOSTER

Focus Puller SEAN CONNOR

Clapper/Loaders NEIL BROWN, MADS THOMSEN, IAN HANSEN

Grip and Helicopter THOMAS KRISTENSEN

Grip HENRY WILLIAMS

Electricians NIELS DOSE, FRANK OMØ, PHILIPPE KRESS

Property Master BRITTA REHN

Prop Man ESBEN MOURIER

Makeup and Hair BARBARA GRUNDMANN

Safety Guide, Greenland THOMAS ULRICH, ERNST MICHEL

Production Runner MADS N. MARSTRAND

Third Unit

Director of Photography
JAN WEINCKE
Focus Pullers
JENS SCHLOSSER,
ERIK THAL-JANTZEN,
BIRGER BOHM
Clapper/Loaders JOHN
FRIMANN RASMUSSEN,
THOMAS HOLM
CHRISTENSEN
Sound Engineer
HENRIK LANGKILDE
Costumes
FRANCOISE NICOLET,
LULU LÜCKOW

Post Production

Post-Production Supervisor
STEPHANIE HÖRMANN
Post-Production Assistant
STEPHANIE WAGNER
2nd Editor PERNILLE
BECH-CHRISTENSEN
AVID Consultant
PETER ENGLESSON
Editing Assistants
NICOLAJ MONBERG,
MICHA SCHÖDEL,
RIKKE SELIN,
MARGIT WILTSCHKO
Editing Trainee
SIMONE LO CHIATTO
Off-Line Editors MOGENS
H. CHRISTIANSEN,
MIRIAM NØRGAARD,
TRINE ANDERSEN,
METTE SCHRAMM,
JILL BYRNIT
Supervising Sound Design
FRIEDRICH M. DOSCH
Sound Designer ANDRÉ
BENDOCCHI-ALVES
Sound Editing Assistant
SILVANA ZAFOSNIK-JAKOB
Sound Editing Trainee
JOAO DA COSTA PINTO
Dialogue Editors EVI
CLAUDIUS, NICK LOWE

Assistant Dialogue Editor
BJØRN OLE SCHROEDER
Foley Editor
CLAUDIA FRÖHLICH
Foley Artists JOO FÜRST,
ANDI SCHNEIDER
Rerecording Mixer
MICHAEL KRANZ
ADR / Foley Mixer STEPHAN
FANDRYCH, HUBERTUS
RATH, JOHN BATEMAN
Engineering
HANS HOHENWARTER
AVID Technician
RUDI NEUBER
Dolby consultant
HUBERT HENLE
Titles designed by
SICKERT
Laboratory BAVARIA
KOPIERWERK GmbH
Sound Stages BAVARIA
FILM GmbH,
TV1 PRODUCTIONS ApS
Visual Effects by Cinesite:
Visual Effects Supervisor
BRAD KUEHN
Head of Production
MITZI GALLAGHER
Production Manager
GIL GAGNON
Visual Effects Producer
JIM LIVOLSI
Composite Supervisor
BOB LYSS
Digital Concept Director
LUBO CHRISTOFF
Digital Compositors NICOLE
PULLEY, MARIO PEIXOTO,
JOHN HARDWICK,
MARK NETTLETON,
BARNEY ROBSON
3-D Animators
PAT CONRAN,
DAVE CHILDS
Digital Matte Painter
CHARLES DARBY
Digital Effects Editor
ROD BASHAM
Production Coordinator
MARTIN HOBBS

Production Assistant
MELISSA DARBY
Camera Equipment
PANAVISION LTD
*Completion Guaranty
supplied by*
INTERNATIONAL FILM
GUARANTORS, INC.
Insurance Services provided by
NEAR NORS INSURANCE
BROKERAGE OF
CALIFORNIA, INC.
Financial Services provided by
BERLINER BANK AG and
BAYRISCHE HYPOTHEKEN
UND WECHSEL BANK AG.
Business and Legal Affairs
MARSHA METZ
Legal Counsel
MATHIAS SCHWARZ,
GEORGE HAYUM,
MICHAEL HAVEMANN
Music Consultant
GEORGE NASCHKE
Stock Footage provided by:
Alaska Stock Agency,
David Hoffmann, Antarctica
Museum of Science and
Industry Photographs used
from: *Color Atlas of Tropical
Medicine and Parasitology*,
4th ed. Published by Mosby-
Wolfe Ltd, London, U.K.
Courtesy of Prof. Wallace
Peters, Prof. Herbert M.
Gilles, Dr. A.J. Duggan, and
Dr. Ralph Muller

The Producers wish to thank:
PROF. VAGN BUCHWALD,
CLAES FELLÄNDER,
RUSSEL FISCHER,
JUKKAS AB,
MERETE RIES,
FRED SPECKTOR,
DANISH
METEOROLOGICAL
INSTITUTE,
MONA JENSEN

This film is a German-Danish-
Swedish coproduction of
Constantin Film Produktion
GmbH in cooperation with
Smilla Film A/S, Greenland
Film Production AB, and
Bavaria Film GmbH.

This film was supported by
Eurimages, the Danish Film
Institute; Hans Hansen, and
the Nordic Film- & TV Fund
and was made with the
participation of FFA and
FilmFernsehFonds Bayern.

Country of First Publication:
Germany

Constantin Film Production
GmbH and its affiliates are the
authors of this motion picture
for the purposes of the Berne
convention and all national
laws giving effect thereto.

The animals used in this film
were in no way mistreated
and all scenes in which they
appeared were under strict
supervision with the utmost
concern for their handling.

Dolby Digital
Panavision

EXT. GREENLAND. ICE FLOES—DUSK

Moving shapes; no scale, but we gradually realize that we're gliding around colossal ICEBERGS, huge floating monoliths—implacable crystal cathedrals that shine like opaline glass. We drift through these towers of ice as a blizzard begins to rage, blowing snow in all directions, and drowning out the beautiful ancient Greenlandic chanting that we have been hearing over.

> *TITLE: 1859—DAVIS STRAIT*

Up ahead, a tiny black speck stands out: a fur-clad Inuit HUNTER poised above a small opening in the ice—so still he seems as frozen as the landscape. A timeless image; this could be present day—or a thousand years ago. Beyond him is a vast wall of ice where a glacier meets the sea.

Closer now, and we see he holds a raised harpoon in one hand, while scratching the ice with another. A team of HUSKIES lies nearby on the ice, harnessed to a primitive sled. They're almost invisible: totally still, caked in snow, and curled into balls to conserve heat.

The hunter drags the tip of his harpoon across

the ice, the sound inaudible beneath the howling wind. Then a faint flicker on the distant horizon. Brief, primordial fear stirs in the dogs' eyes—but the hunter keeps gazing at the hole.

EXT. UNDERWATER—ICE POOL—DUSK

A sudden, eerie silence. We're under the ice—as we look up, everything's a startling blue. All we hear now is the echo of the hunter's harpoon, scratching against the ice above us. The dark shadow of a seal glides through the icy water . . .

EXT. GREENLAND. ICE FLOES—TWILIGHT

The hunter slowly raises his harpoon—then another flicker of light on the horizon, brighter this time, followed by an ominous crackling sound, like a distant forest fire. The huskies strain at their harnesses; the hunter's eyes betray incipient fear. Suddenly the entire sky lights up, brighter than a thousand suns. A titanic explosion shreds the horizon beyond the glacier cliff, vaporizing the ice. Another rumble. The ice floe shudders. The hunter turns to see what looks like a white curtain rising from the glacier—a curtain that starts to billow down the valley toward us. He abandons his kill and leaps to his sled, cracking his dogs into action.

Faster and faster they race, desperately seeking escape. But the ice floe is beginning to break up. The hunter turns, his terrified eyes briefly catching sight of the avalanche of pulverized snow before he—and we—are engulfed in a white cloud of death.

FADE TO WHITE.
INT. MICROSCOPE POINT OF VIEW—SFX

From out of the whiteness, a single crystal of ice begins to form, and a symmetrical snowflake grows before our eyes. We hear a click, very close to us.

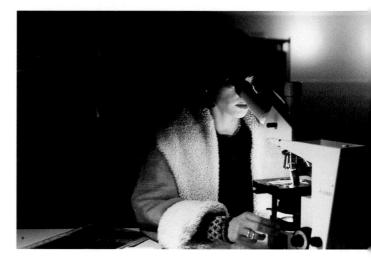

TITLE:
FRONT CREDITS
As the snowflake forms, so it breeds others in an exquisite chain reaction of hexagonal lattices . . .

INT. LAB—DAY

A woman, SMILLA JASPERSEN, studies the growing crystals through a camera attached to a microscope, linked to a small deep-freeze unit. Mid-thirties, cool, striking. She pauses to make a few notes. No visible reaction to the beauty of her studies—she is as cool and remote as her subject.

THROUGH THE MICROSCOPE: Now the snow crystal begins to sprout feelers: sharp spears that blossom as they extend outward, to meet up with a dozen more crystals that suddenly pop into existence. Another click.

We pull back to show Smilla sitting alone in a small cubicle of the lab. Others work nearby in similar isolation; this is not a workplace where people know one another, simply anonymous rented space. Smilla turns off the microscope,

(ABOVE) *Just before the shooting of Isaiah lying dead in the snow, Bille August checks that Clipper lies in the right position, and the last "bloodstains" are applied*

gathers her things, puts on a heavy shearling coat. Greets no one on her way out.

COPENHAGEN—PRESENT TIME

EXT. COPENHAGEN—DUSK

The city seen from above. Christmas decorations light up the dark blue dusk hour. The harbor is frozen, the rooftops are covered with freshly fallen snow, giving the scene a kind of pre-holiday winter melancholy.

EXT. KNIPPELS BRIDGE—DUSK

Smilla crosses the bridge spanning the frozen harbor. Shoppers hurry home carrying presents and Christmas trees. Smilla's arms are filled with packages. It's really snowing now. We hear the sound of an ambulance off in the distance.

Smilla hears it getting closer, then turns to see it crossing the bridge and turning into her street. Smilla walks faster, breaks into a run.

EXT. THE WHITE PALACE—DUSK

The WHITE PALACE, the nickname for the apartment complex where Smilla lives. A crowd of curious onlookers has gathered in front of her building, where an area has been cordoned off. The ambulance has arrived, along with two police cars. Smilla tries to push through the crowd—is stopped by a POLICEMAN who will not let her through.

She pushes her way through, frantic now, a package of oranges spilling from her arms and one of them rolling into the blood that stains the snow. It's coming from the head of ISAIAH, a six-year-old, who lies with his legs tucked up under him, his face in the snow, and his hands around his head, as if he were shielding himself from the spotlight shining on him—and as if the snow were a window through which he had caught sight of something deep inside the earth.

Smilla moans, comes close to him. He is not dressed properly for winter, is wearing a thin T-shirt, jeans, and rubber rain pants over the jeans. Smilla can't stop staring at the worn soles of his basketball sneakers. We can see she is willing herself not to fall apart.

Just then, two more policemen escort Isaiah's mother, JULIANE, out of the building. It takes two of them to hold her up: she is drunk, wailing with incoherent grief when she sees her son lying dead in the snow. As Smilla approaches her, we see she is pure Inuit, with once beautiful Eskimo features ravaged by years of chronic drinking . . . Smilla embraces her; Juliane leans against her.

JULIANE
My baby . . . Why, Smilla?

SMILLA
Juliane . . .
Smilla holds her for a long moment as the ambulance drivers lift Isaiah from the snow and place him on a stretcher.

EXT. COPENHAGEN—DAY (FLASHBACK)

Smilla and Isaiah play in the snow.

EXT. WHITE PALACE—DUSK

Smilla hands Juliane back to the policemen. They take her over to a nearby bench. Smilla turns to the one still keeping the crowd back.

POLICEMAN
He was playing on the roof. He fell.
Smilla looks up at the adjacent building. She stands up and crosses toward the building.

(ABOVE) At the start of the writing process, Peter Høeg tried to write a new beginning for the story. Here are a couple of his handwritten pages

EXT. ROOFTOP—DUSK

*As Smilla exits the stairwell to the roof, she sees a
DETECTIVE, imperious, hard-looking, and a
PHOTOGRAPHER, using a Polaroid camera with
a flash to photograph Isaiah's footprints. They
appear in the snow as if they are being photographed by a special lens. They head diagonally
toward the edge where Isaiah jumped. Smilla turns
to see the MECHANIC behind her.*

MECHANIC
I f-f-found him . . .

SMILLA
What made him run?

DETECTIVE
Who are you?

SMILLA
I'm the lady who lived upstairs from him.
(Gesturing to the Mechanic)
He's the gentleman from the ground floor.

DETECTIVE
You're not allowed up here.
*He watches the photographer as he changes
cameras.*

DETECTIVE
(To photographer)
Only the footprints of the deceased . . .
I don't know why the hell he was playing up here—
running around wild without supervision.

SMILLA
Strange way to play, don't you think?

DETECTIVE
(To photographer)
Take these people downstairs.

SMILLA
The tracks go in a straight line toward the edge. No
child in the world would play like that.
*As Smilla reenters the hatch to the stairwells she
manages to get a good look at the footprints.*

INT. JULIANE'S APARTMENT—NIGHT

*Smilla is sitting at the kitchen table with Juliane. It
is filthy: dirty dishes, ashtrays overflowing. A bottle
of cheap apple wine on the table. Juliane is blitzed.*

JULIANE
Why so many accidents, Smilla?
(She begins to cry.)
. . . First my husband and now my baby. Why,
Smilla?

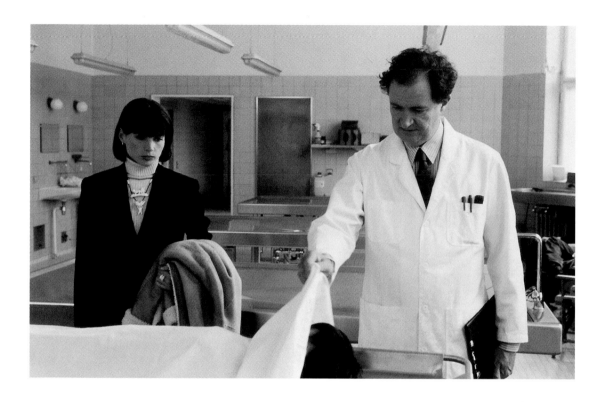

SMILLA
I don't know.

JULIANE
How am I going to go to the morgue tomorrow?

SMILLA
If they think it's an accident, why are they doing an autopsy?

JULIANE
(Shrugs.)
They told me to show up, sign papers, and get his things.

SMILLA
I'll go, Juliane. Let me go.

INT. MORGUE—DAY

Smilla stands in front of the body of Isaiah, covered with a sheet.

A redheaded, distracted pathologist, LAGER-MANN, has shown her into the autopsy room. He hesitates before pulling back the sheet. Then he does, exposing Isaiah to her.

SMILLA
I'm not his mother . . . We were friends . . .
Silence. Smilla looks at Isaiah on the cold steel table.

DISSOLVE TO:
INT. WHITE PALACE. STAIRWAY—DAY (FLASHBACK)

The end of a brutally hot summer's day. Smilla pokes her head out from her apartment, still holding the book she has been reading. She sees Isaiah, bouncing a ball on the steps. He is filthy, dressed in his underpants and sneakers.

SMILLA
Beat it, you little shit.
When he doesn't move:

SMILLA
(Same thing in Greenlandic)
Peerit.
He is taken aback. He sees the book in her hands.

ISAIAH
Will you read me a story?

SMILLA
(Mimicking his childish voice)
No, I won't read you a story.

SMILLA
I had hoped he would have a long life.
Lagermann walks around the table while he looks at the boy.

LAGERMANN
Yes. All parents hope that for their children. I have children of my own. I know how you must feel. My deepest condolences.

INT. SMILLA'S APARTMENT—DAY (FLASHBACK CONT.)

She goes back into her apartment, slams the door. Starts to read again from the book she has been holding that prompted his asking her to read: Euclid's Elements. *The doorbell rings. Smilla goes to answer it.*

INT. WHITE PALACE. STAIRWAY—EVENING (FLASHBACK CONT.)

Smilla opens the door. Isaiah is standing there.

SMILLA
Persistent little bastard, aren't you?
He continues to wait.
I can't be your little friend, okay? I have nothing to offer you. Just go away.
He continues to stand there, implacable, polite.

SMILLA
Look, there's absolutely no future in this.
When he still doesn't move, she steps aside, letting him enter. He goes directly to her sofa, sits, and crosses his legs. Impeccable manners. Waits for her to read to him. Thinking this will get rid of him, she starts to read from Euclid's Elements.

SMILLA
"A point is that which cannot be divided. A line is a length without breadth."
Smilla looks at him.
This can't possibly interest you . . .
But he doesn't budge. Smilla continues to read.
"A semicircle is a figure contained within a diameter . . . and the circumference intersected by the diameter."
After a moment, she is quiet. They both sit in silence.

SMILLA
You smell bad.
He doesn't say anything.
. . . I don't mean to say this to hurt your feelings, but you stink.

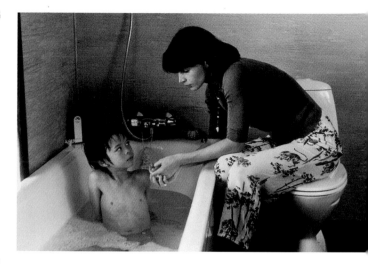

INT. SMILLA'S APARTMENT. BATHROOM— NIGHT

Isaiah is naked in the bathtub. Smilla is rubbing his back with a sponge. He is enjoying it.

SMILLA
What interests you?
No one has ever asked him a question like this in his life. He's thinking about it . . .

SMILLA
Do you know anything about Greenland?
He shrugs.

SMILLA
You should know something about where you're from.

ISAIAH
Why?

SMILLA
Because it tells you who you are. It's important to know who you are.

ISAIAH
Do you know who you are?

SMILLA
No . . .

ISAIAH
Did your mom read you stories?

SMILLA
She told me stories.

ISAIAH
About what?

SMILLA
About Greenland . . . When she used to hunt . . . Stories like that.

**EXT. ZOO—DAY
(FLASHBACK CONT.)**

They are watching a polar bear as it does figure eights in a small body of water. It's heartbreaking.

ISAIAH
Miss Smilla, can we go home?

SMILLA
Why, are you tired?

ISAIAH
No, home to Greenland.
She turns to look at him.

SMILLA
What do you want me to do, lie to you? Tell you

we'll go to Greenland and then not go? Get your hopes up?

INT. NATIONAL MUSEUM—DAY (FLASHBACK CONT.)

Smilla and Isaiah are in the huge, dark rooms, looking at the Greenland exhibits. It is summer. She wears a dress; he wears shorts and his sneakers, is feverish with excitement. He runs from room to room filled with kayaks and umiaks, polar bears, seal skins, harpoons, ancient sunglasses made from ivory. They stop in front of a case that shows two tribes fighting. Smilla reads from the side of the case:

SMILLA
"If Inuits who are feuding wish to reconcile they touch each other's breast, saying, '*Ilaga . . . Ilaga . . .*'"

ISAIAH
Ilaga . . .

SMILLA
It means "friend" . . . *Ilaga . . .*

INT. MORGUE—DAY

Smilla is lost in this reverie. Lagermann has moved away from her, approaches now as he sees her thoughts return to the room, to Isaiah lying before her.

LAGERMANN
When a child dies like that, it's a tragedy. A terrible accident.

SMILLA
It wasn't an accident.

LAGERMANN
(Studies her.)
I see.

SMILLA
Who did the autopsy?

LAGERMANN
It was routine.

SMILLA
That's not what I asked you.

LAGERMANN
Dr. Loyen.

SMILLA
Johannes Loyen? Isn't he the head of the Institute for Arctic Medicine?

LAGERMANN
Yes.
Lagermann is extremely uncomfortable.

SMILLA
Why would such a famous man do an autopsy on a six-year-old?

LAGERMANN
It was routine.

SMILLA
So you've said.
He walks her to the door now, has to go back to work. Hesitates, wants to give her something, finally hands her his card.

LAGERMANN
I'm so sorry for your loss.
Smilla nods, has nothing further to say to him.

INT. WHITE PALACE. STAIRWAY—NIGHT

Smilla is climbing the stairs to her apartment when the Mechanic steps out of his ground-floor apartment. Smilla stops and regards him. He is very shy, can barely look at her.

SMILLA
Do you think his feet were cold?
The Mechanic looks at her.

SMILLA
He always wore those sneakers. When I saw him lying there in the snow—the soles were so run-down. His feet must have been cold.

MECHANIC
Would you like something to drink?

SMILLA
I may be from Greenland, but I don't drink.
He nods. Wants to extend some kindness to her . . .

MECHANIC
Are you hungry?

SMILLA
Look, I don't want to share anything with you, okay?

MECHANIC
Okay. Perhaps you can sleep. G-g-goodnight.

SMILLA
Do you always stutter?

MECHANIC
No.

SMILLA
I make you nervous, then?
He doesn't answer her, just regards her steadily.

SMILLA
Don't you think I see the way you look at me?
She can't stop, all her grief turning into pure vitriol.

SMILLA
What'd you think—we'd get drunk and fuck all night, fueled by our mutual grief? Is that what you thought?
Dead silence. After a long beat:

MECHANIC
It's okay, Smilla. I loved him, too.
The absolute dogged kindness of this kills her. She covers her mouth with shame, as if to prevent any other words of insult from escaping her.

SMILLA
(Whispering)
Yes, of course you did.
She runs up the stairs, filled with shame and embarrassment.

<table>
<tr><td colspan="6" align="center">SMILLA'S SENSE OF SNOW</td></tr>
<tr><td colspan="6" align="center">CONSTANTIN FILM PRODUKTION GMBH</td></tr>
<tr><td colspan="6" align="center">CALL SHEET NO: 18</td></tr>
</table>

PRODUCTION OFFICE:	CREW HOTEL:	MOBILEPHONES:
SMILLA FILM A/S	HOTEL ASCOT	EMMA: 20 22 37 93
SKUDEHAVNSVEJ 5	STUDIESTRÆDE 81	MOUNS: 40 51 31 93
2100 COPENHAGEN Ø	1554 COPENHAGEN V	MARIANNE C.: 40 13 17 03
TEL. 70 20 21 02	TEL. 33 12 60 00	THOMAS H.: 40 11 21 74
FAX: 70 20 21 03	TEL. 33 14 60 40	GARY: +44 468 49 00 35

DIRECTOR: BILLE AUGUST   PRODUCERS: BERND EICHINGER
                                            MARTIN MOSZKOWICZ

DATE: Tuesday 26th March 1996   UNIT CALL: 09.00

SUNRISE: 06.08   BREAKFAST AT LOC. 1: 08.45
                                             LUNCH: 13.30

SUNSET: 18.44   WRAP: 19.00

LOCATION: UNIT BASE:

1.   Landbohøjskole, Bülowsvej 13, 1870 Frb. C   Bülowsvej 13, 1870 Frb. C

TODAYS WEATHER:

Dry with sun. Temperature between 3 - 6 celcius. The wind will be light to fresh around north.

SCENE SET		INT/EXT	D/N	PAGES	CAST NO.
23	Stairs outer office Arctic Medicine INT (Smilla enters outer office)		DAY	1/8	1
24	Loyens office (Smilla questions Loyen)	INT	DAY	2 5/8	1, 5

CAST NO.	ARTIST	CHARACTER	PICK UP	WR/MU	ON SET
1	Julia Ormond	Smilla	07.30	07.45	09.30
5	Tom Wilkinson	Loyen	08.30	08.45	09.45

STAND INS / DBLS / STUNTS			WR/MU	ON SET
Kim Samson	Miss Ormond			09.00
Thomas Rasmussen	Utility			09.00

EXTRAS / AS PER TOVE BERG BRAMSEN			WR/MU	ON SET
23	2 x doctors men - rpt. to unit base		09.00	
	1 x doctors woman - rpt. to unit base		09.00	
24	Secretary - rpt. to unit base		09.00	

(ABOVE AND FOLLOWING PAGES) After every day's work the call sheet for the next day is handed out. Here the crew members find all the information about which scenes are going to be shot, when crew and cast have to be on the set, which special equipment and props are necessary, etc.

INT. INSTITUTE FOR ARCTIC MEDICINE. STAIRWAY—DAY

Smilla walks up the stairs and disappears behind a huge glass door. A sign on it tells us this is the office of PROFESSOR J. LOYEN.

INT. LOYEN'S OFFICE—DAY

Enormous, the size of a tennis court—an astounding view of the park. LOYEN, a tanned fit man in his fifties, sits behind his desk, facing Smilla. He studies her.

SMILLA
Dr. Loyen . . .

LOYEN
You're of Greenlandic descent?

SMILLA
My mother was from Thule.
(Changing subject)
You were the one who examined Isaiah?

LOYEN
Yes.

SMILLA
What I would like to know is: what did he die of?

LOYEN
He fell from a height of five stories. The organism as a whole quite simply collapses.

SMILLA
Was there any trace of violence?

LOYEN
None at all. What makes you think that?
She ignores his question.

SMILLA
Is it possible to see the autopsy report?

LOYEN
You wouldn't understand it.
Smilla doesn't say anything. Loyen starts to feel uncomfortable with the vacuum. His voice takes on a soothing tone.

LOYEN
Look . . . both we and the police are interested in the most thorough investigation possible. In a case like this, if there is even the slightest doubt—we look for everything. And we find everything. A child defends itself and gets skin cells under its nails. There was nothing like that. Nothing at all. We looked at the police report, and the footprints show quite clearly that the boy was alone on the roof before he fell.
Smilla regards him closely now.

LOYEN
There was no indication that this was anything but an accident. It's tragic, of course, but the case is closed.
Smilla still says nothing.

LOYEN
Please drop by again, my dear lady, if there's anything else that troubles you . . .
Smilla gets up and walks toward the door. She stops, turns around.

SMILLA
I'm filing a complaint with the district attorney.

LOYEN
(Weary)
What makes this your business?

SMILLA
A six-year-old boy was murdered. I'm making it my business.

LOYEN
(Angry now)
I've told you, there was no forensic evidence to indicate any foul play. None whatsoever.

SMILLA
I don't care about your forensic evidence. I knew him. That's my evidence . . .
. . . We all have our phobias.
Do you know what Isaiah's was? It was heights.
A long pause before Loyen answers.

LOYEN
Nevertheless, he *was* up there.

SMILLA
Yes. He was. And what puzzles me, what keeps me awake at night, is wondering what made him go up there at all.
And, without looking at him again, Smilla leaves.

INT. SMILLA'S APARTMENT—NIGHT (FLASHBACK)

It is very late. Smilla is pacing, overwhelmed with guilt. The doorbell rings.
  Smilla goes to answer it and reveals Isaiah. There is something in his face that forces her to remain quiet. With the utmost dignity he asks:

ISAIAH
May I please spend the night?
Below them they hear the sound of breaking glass and people screaming in Greenlandic. Smilla looks back at Isaiah; she sees the shame on his face.

INT. SMILLA'S APARTMENT. BEDROOM— NIGHT (FLASHBACK)

Smilla lies next to him in her bed, watches him sleep. There is a red welt on his neck. Smilla brushes his hair back to look at it. At his next exhale, she leans in close to him, looks as if she is going to kiss him. Instead, she inhales the air he just expelled—so in love with him she must bring some essence of him into herself.

INT. SMILLA'S APARTMENT—NIGHT

CUT TO: These words appear on a computer screen, as they are being typed out:

  COPENHAGEN. DEC. 15, 1996. TO THE ATTORNEY GENERAL. MY NAME IS SMILLA JASPERSEN AND I WISH TO FILE A COMPLAINT.

We pull back to show Smilla sitting at the computer. She is listening to Beethoven's violin concerto.

She is very agitated. She looks across the room to where Isaiah mostly sat. Goes back to her typing. Looks up again.

EXT. LAGERMANN'S HOUSE—NIGHT

Smilla rings the doorbell, waits. Five people open the door at once, all of them children, of all ages— all of them redheaded, covered with flour. A tall WOMAN, also redheaded, appears behind them.

REDHEADED WOMAN
We're going to miss the film. You're late. I called the agency twice.
And behind her, Lagermann, who sees Smilla now.

LAGERMANN
(To his wife)
She's not the sitter, dear. Come in . . .
He does not seem surprised to see Smilla appear out of nowhere at his home—it's almost as if he'd some-how been expecting her. Gestures for her to come in and to follow him.

INT. LAGERMANN'S GREENHOUSE— NIGHT

The greenhouse is filled with thousands of cacti, lit by ultraviolet grow lights. A table and chairs. Lagermann lights a cigar, draws on it greedily.

LAGERMANN
We get a thousand cases a year. I can't be expected to remember every single one.
He stops.

SMILLA
Unburden yourself, Lagermann. You'll feel better.
Lagermann is silent for another moment, makes up his mind, nods yes.

LAGERMANN
We were very busy the night he was brought in. Drunk drivers and Christmas parties. You're not squeamish, are you?

SMILLA
No . . .

CUT TO:
INT. MORGUE—NIGHT (FLASHBACK)

A scene from hell. In the autopsy room, three or four pathologists are at work at examination tables. Lagermann is examining Isaiah.

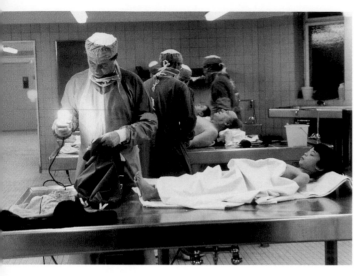

LAGERMANN (VOICE-OVER)
I have a little trick. The kind of thing you invent in any profession.

INT. LAGERMANN'S GREENHOUSE—NIGHT

LAGERMANN
I hold a light bulb inside the pant legs. Near the thigh, there's a perforation.

INT. MORGUE—NIGHT (FLASHBACK)

We see Lagermann holding up the pants and putting the light bulb inside them. We see the hole in the fabric.

LAGERMANN (VOICE-OVER)
I examine the boy again. All of this is routine. Then I find a hole in his thigh. There's no bleeding and the tissue hasn't contracted. Do you know what that means?

INT. LAGERMANN'S GREENHOUSE—NIGHT

SMILLA
No.

LAGERMANN
It means that whatever happened at that spot occurred *after* his heart stopped beating.

EXT. AMBULANCE—NIGHT (FLASHBACK)

As it races through the night, a black Volvo pulls alongside it suddenly, and then overtakes it, causing it to pull over.

INT. MORGUE—NIGHT (FLASHBACK)

We see what Lagermann describes.

LAGERMANN (VOICE-OVER)
I take a closer look at his trousers. There's a little indentation around the hole. This rings a bell. So I get out a biopsy needle. A kind of syringe, quite big, attached to a handle.

INT. DESERTED HOSPITAL CORRIDOR—NIGHT (FLASHBACK)

We see the back of Loyen walking down the dimly lit corridor. He opens the door to the mortuary waiting area to see Isaiah's body on a gurney. He goes inside, closes the door behind him.

LAGERMANN (VOICE-OVER)
You plunge it into the tissue to get a sample. The hole in his trousers was where someone who was in a hurry shoved it in with a good whack.

INT. MORTUARY WAITING AREA—
NIGHT (FLASHBACK)

Loyen's hands prepare the biopsy needle. He moves the sheet to reveal Isaiah.

INT. LAGERMANN'S GREENHOUSE—
NIGHT

LAGERMANN
Someone took a muscle biopsy from him *after* he died.

SMILLA
The ambulance drivers?

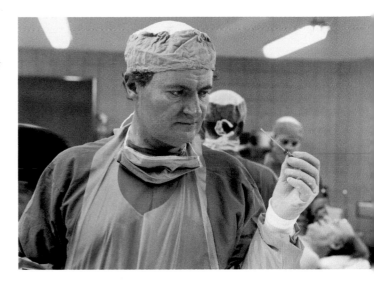

LAGERMANN
I talked to the driver and the medics and the order-lies who received the body. They all swore on a stack of Bibles they didn't do it.

SMILLA
Why didn't Loyen tell me this?
Lagermann shrugs.
Smilla sits quietly, digesting this.

LAGERMANN
I was about to start the autopsy when Loyen arrived. He was surprised I'd started on the boy. He pulled me off it and took over.
(Beat)
What do you think was after him on the roof?

SMILLA
I don't know. But I won't be much in the Christmas spirit until I find out.
Lagermann gets up.

LAGERMANN
Please don't come here again.
Smilla nods, gets up to leave.

LAGERMANN
One more thing . . .
The night he died wasn't the first time I'd seen him.
Smilla waits.

LAGERMANN
. . . He came in once a month. Loyen examined him. Alone.

SMILLA
I don't suppose there are any records?

LAGERMANN
I already looked. Nothing.

CUT TO:
EXT. CEMETERY—DAY

Isaiah's small coffin is slowly being lowered into the grave. It's snowing, the thick hexagonal flakes the same shape as the small wood casket. A PASTOR is

tries to hand Juliane an envelope. Smilla watches as Juliane refuses to take it and moves off. When he follows her and continues to try to give it to her, she spits in his face. He stands frozen; the other man moves forward. The white-haired man holds him back, pulls out a handkerchief, wipes his face off, as Juliane walks away with her friends. The two men move toward a dark blue Mercedes.

INT. JULIANE'S APARTMENT—DAY

Smilla enters the room, Juliane, almost incoherent now with drink, sits with some Inuit friends drinking. When she sees Smilla she gets up.

SMILLA
Who was that man at the funeral? What was he trying to give you?

JULIANE
I don't want his money no more. Dirty fucking money, Smilla.

SMILLA
What money? Why does he give you money?

JULIANE
They always try to buy me off, Smilla. First my husband and now my kid.

SMILLA
Who's "they"?
Juliane goes over to a drawer and pulls out a greasy manila envelope stuffed with papers. She begins to search through it. The detritus of an immigrant's life: receipts for the gas and phone bills, slips from the alcohol clinic, test results for sexually transmitted diseases. A receipt book of stubs for a monthly pension.
And a letter—dated June 1993 and bearing the very distinctive seal of Greenland Mining.

saying the prayers.
Smilla, crying for the first time since Isaiah's death, stands off to one side by herself. The Mechanic is behind her, lost in his own grief. She is shivering, suddenly feels the weight of the Mechanic's large coat draped over her. She nods in gratitude, won't look at him directly.
We pull up to see Juliane, drunk, wailing, falling to the ground as the coffin is lowered.

EXT. CEMETERY—DAY

The service is over. Three Inuit friends pick up Juliane and start to lead her off.
Smilla watches now as an important-looking man with white hair in a ponytail approaches Juliane. Another man is at his side, both of them conspicuous at this very small gathering of a few mourners.
Smilla can't hear what the white-haired man is saying to Juliane, but he looks as if he's trying to express his deepest sympathy. At the same time, he

There was real snow on the ground, but in the burial scene a lot of falling snow was needed. The snow guns took care of that

JULIANE
(Reading letter)
"We wish to inform you that the directors of Greenland Mining have decided to grant you a widow's pension following the death of your husband, Norsaq Christiansen."
But she's too drunk to continue. She hands it to Smilla, who continues reading it. In the margin she sees a handwritten note: "I'm so sorry. Elsa Lübing."

SMILLA
It's signed Elsa Lübing. Who's she? Who is Elsa Lübing? Can I take this?
Juliane shrugs.

CUT TO:

16 mm footage transferred to video: the following images appear on the television screen. The images have the grainy appearance of film shot many years ago.

Huskie dog team appears in frame, exhausted, pulling a sled, the dogs panting after a long journey. A beautiful INUIT WOMAN steps off the sled, laughs at the camera, as dogs bark and jump around, ecstatic to be home.

MORITZ (VOICE-OVER)
Oh, yes . . . I filmed this as you came back from a hunting trip with your mother.
The woman goes to the front of the sled and unties a very small child who is strapped to the front of it.

MORITZ (VOICE-OVER)
You'd had very bad weather, with a lot of fog. You were lost. Everyone had given up hope. Your mother said you suddenly pointed, with complete conviction. You knew the way home. No one could explain it.
The woman and child, red-faced, happy, wave to the camera, and begin to unload the seals they have hunted. We still don't see the man who is talking, but it is almost as if he is doing this recitation by rote—as he's done it many times before.

MORITZ (VOICE-OVER)
From that day on, they always strapped you to the front of the sled whenever they went on a hunting trip.

INT. MORITZ'S HOUSE. LIVING ROOM— DAY

Close-up Smilla: as she watches herself on the screen with her mother. Like the man, she seems oddly hypnotized by the ritual watching of this footage. Smilla sits on a couch next to her father, Moritz—elegant, tanned, dressed in an Hermès suit. They are in his very elegant library.

MORITZ
You knew exactly how to get home.

SMILLA
(Weary)
Yes, Father.

MORITZ
How the hell do you explain that?
Clearly, this ritual pains her.

SMILLA
I don't know. I just knew.

BENJA, Moritz's pouty twenty-four-year-old girl-friend, sits on the couch next to him. She wears leotards and leg warmers, with a chiffon miniskirt tied around her perfect ass, and she is massaging her feet. She takes the remote control from the table and stops the video. Moritz tries to grab her hand with the remote control, but she takes it away from him.

BENJA
You were a regular little Eagle Scout . . .
A real little Nanook of the North.

MORITZ
Cut it out, Benja.

SMILLA
You should try Brentan . . .

BENJA
What . . . ?

SMILLA
Brentan, for fungus between the toes . . .

BENJA
It's not fungus. People don't get that till they reach your age . . .

SMILLA
Yes, adolescents do, too, especially if they work out a lot, and it spreads to the crotch quite easily . . .
Benja gets up and leaves. Smilla turns to Moritz.

SMILLA
What do you know about Johannes Loyen?

MORITZ
A very talented man. He created the Institute for Arctic Medicine.

SMILLA
What's his interest in forensic medicine?

MORITZ
He started out as a pathologist.

SMILLA
He did an autopsy on a six-year-old boy.

MORITZ
It must have been a good career move.
Moritz gets up, goes to his collection of books. He extracts a weighty tome: Mesozoan Organisms: Their Genealogy and Evolution, *by Johannes Loyen. He hands it to Smilla, who leafs through it.*

MORITZ
Since our school days Loyen has always wanted to be recognized as the best in the world. Not just in Denmark but in the universe. And it wasn't just a flame, like in the rest of us, it was a conflagration. This tome was his thesis for his professorial degree . . .

SMILLA
Mesozoan parasites—what are they?

MORITZ
Prehistoric worms.

INT. MORITZ'S HOUSE. HALLWAY—DAY

Moritz walks Smilla to the door, helps her into a heavy fur coat. Benja lingers, happy Smilla is leaving.

SMILLA
Write me a prescription, Father.

MORITZ
(Alarmed)
Are you sick, Smilla?

SMILLA
With this piece of paper you can save my life and keep your Hippocratic oath. It has to be five figures.
He hesitates. Smilla explains.
I let someone down. A child—it'll take money to do something about it.

He sighs deeply, says nothing, then goes to get his checkbook in the next room.

MORITZ
I'm afraid that check won't be nearly enough.

BENJA
He only gives you money because you make him feel so guilty. He told me that.

SMILLA
And he only gives you money, Benja, because you are such an amusing little fuck. But one day, like all of us, you'll wake up and your perfect tits will be starting to sag and your perfect little piquant ass will be starting to go. Then what, Benja?

BENJA
Then you'll be dead, Smilla, and I won't care.
Moritz returns, hands Smilla a check.

MORITZ
Come for Christmas dinner, Smilla.

SMILLA
I don't celebrate Christmas. It doesn't mean anything to me.
She takes the check from his hand.

INT. BUS—NIGHT

Smilla is on her way home on a bus leaving the suburbs. There are not many passengers at this late hour. The steady rhythm of the bus makes Smilla sleepy, and she closes her eyes . . .

INT. SMILLA'S APARTMENT—NIGHT (FLASHBACK)

Smilla sits in the sofa next to Isaiah and reads to him. On the table in front of them are his knife and some suction cups.

SMILLA
". . . They hunted seals by their igloos, they stalked them with screens on the ice . . ."
She looks up, Isaiah has turned his body to face her, to follow her face with his eyes.
". . . They waited for them on the floe edge and they harpooned them from kayaks . . ."
He has turned again.
". . . They hunted them in the bluish darkness of the winter night . . ."
And once more he has turned his body. This time, Smilla grabs him, leans him back into the sofa, and turns away her face so that he cannot see her.

SMILLA
"To the Inuits, the seal was life."
(Beat)
What did I just say? Isaiah, tell me what I just said
. . . Tell me, what did I just say?
Isaiah's face: he is very upset, cannot hear her.

SMILLA
(As a horrible realization sets in)
Oh, my God.
She storms out of her apartment.

**INT. WHITE PALACE. STAIRWAY—NIGHT
(FLASHBACK CONT.)**

Smilla races down the stairs to Juliane's apartment.

**INT. JULIANE'S APARTMENT—NIGHT
(FLASHBACK CONT.)**

*As Smilla bursts in, Juliane lies on the sofa, almost
unconscious with drink.*

SMILLA
Juliane . . .
Isaiah's deaf, Juliane . . .
Juliane is too drunk to comprehend.
He's gone deaf from having three ear infections,
from your not taking care of him . . .
*Juliane looks up at her; she is so drunk she almost
cannot speak.*

JULIANE
The doctors said he was okay . . .

SMILLA
What doctors? Who told you he was okay? He's not
okay!

JULIANE
There's nothing to worry about . . .
*Juliane reaches for a bottle. Smilla lets go of her,
storms out, slamming the door.*

**INT. SMILLA'S APARTMENT—NIGHT
(FLASHBACK CONT.)**

*She comes back in. Isaiah is very upset, watches her
as she approaches. When she is next to him he takes
his fist and touches her on the chest.*

ISAIAH
Ilaga.

SMILLA
I'm not mad at you.
*He does it again, takes her hand and tries to force it
on his chest.*

ISAIAH
Ilaga.

SMILLA
Stop it! I'm not mad at you.

ISAIAH
Ilaga . . . Ilaga . . .
He won't let her hand go until she says it.

SMILLA
Yes. You're my friend. *Ilaga*, Isaiah.
He comes into her arms. She smooths the hair from his fevered brow.

INT. WHITE PALACE. STAIRWAY—NIGHT

Smilla enters her building, moves past the Mechanic's half-open doorway. She starts up the stairs, trying to be quiet so he doesn't hear her.

INT. SMILLA'S APARTMENT—NIGHT

Smilla opens the door to her apartment, steps in. It is dark inside, lit only by the streetlights outside. Smilla fumbles for the light switch, almost has a heart attack when the lights come on—a cadaverous man in a huge overcoat, RAVN, is sitting in one of her chairs, staring at her.

RAVN
Please, don't be frightened. I'm with the district attorney.

SMILLA
Do you always make house calls?

RAVN
No. Let's just say it's the nature of this case and because of your thought-provoking letter.
She waits; they study each other.

RAVN
I spoke to Professor Loyen. He told me that you came in to see him.

SMILLA
There were tracks in the snow.

RAVN
I read the report and looked at the pictures.

SMILLA
You have to have special lenses and lights or it doesn't show up.

RAVN
What doesn't show up?

SMILLA
There were acceleration tracks. When you take off from the snow or ice, a pronation occurs in the ankle joint. Like when you walk barefoot in the sand. *(She comes close to him, demonstrates with her wrist.)*
If the movement is too fast, not firm enough, there will be a little slip backwards.

RAVN
As with any child who is playing . . .

SMILLA
No, when you're used to playing in the snow, you don't leave that kind of track because the movement is not efficient. He grew up in Greenland. He was used to snow.
(She stops, looks at him.)
You don't believe me.

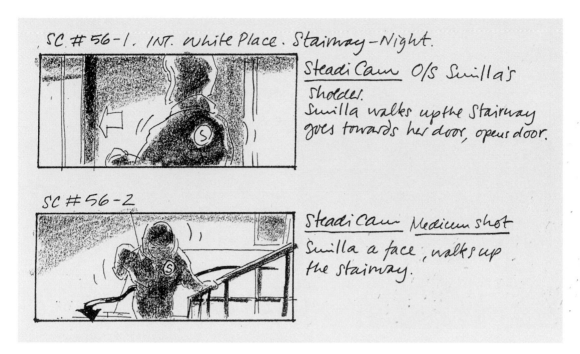

The storyboards are drawings which, like a cartoon, chart the progress of the scene to assist the crew. Danish storyboard artist Simon Bang made storyboards for a great part of the film, following Bille August's directions

RAVN
I didn't say that. The truth is, I felt uncomfortable about this case from the beginning. Then when you wrote the letter, that confirmed it for me. But with so little to go on . . .
(Long beat)
What do you want me to do?

SMILLA
Find out what was after him.
He nods reflectively, stands up.

RAVN
I'll do my best. You have my word.

SMILLA
Thank you. I don't know your name.

RAVN
Ravn . . .

way. Ravn goes past him. He keeps staring at Smilla, wondering who this man is that she hugged. Smilla gives him a dirty look, then slams and locks her door.

INT. SMILLA'S APARTMENT—NIGHT

Smilla leans against her door with relief. And flips open the wallet she lifted from Ravn's pocket. There is one card that catches her eye. She pulls it out of the wallet. It is from Greenland Mining.

Smilla goes over to her desk, gets Juliane's pension letter with Elsa Lübing's note in the margin, and compares the seal on the letterhead with Ravn's card. The seals are identical.

Close-up: the name Elsa Lübing in the phone book.

Smilla rips the page from the book.

EXT. ELSA LÜBING'S BUILDING— EARLY MORNING

Smilla searches for the name E. Lübing next to the intercom. Buzzes it. When a woman's voice answers:

SMILLA
My name's Smilla Jaspersen. I have some questions about Greenland Mining.

LÜBING (VOICE-OVER)
I'm sorry. I can't help you—I don't work there anymore.

Smilla is defeated. Steps back and counts the floors until she is looking at Elsa's balcony on the seventh floor. Her eye then takes in the balcony directly beneath it, covered with potted plants. Smilla goes back to the intercom and buzzes this apartment.

INT. WHITE PALACE. STAIRWAY— NIGHT

They are out on the landing now; he is about to head down the stairs.

RAVN
I'll be in touch.

SMILLA
Thank you, Mr. Ravn.
She hugs him suddenly, surprising him.

SMILLA
Thank you for believing me.
He starts down. Smilla is suddenly aware of the Mechanic, watching her, looking up from his hall-

MRS. SCHOU (VOICE-OVER)
Who is it?

SMILLA
Delivery for Elsa Lübing, from the florist. She isn't
home—would you buzz me in, please?

MRS. SCHOU (VOICE-OVER)
We have strict instructions not to open the door for
nonresidents.

SMILLA
(Reading name off intercom)
These are orchids, Mrs. Schou. They're straight off
the plane from Portugal, and they'll die if I leave
them out here.
Mrs. Schou buzzes her in.

INT. ELSA LÜBING'S HALLWAY—MORNING

Elsa Lübing's door is shut. Smilla can hear the plant
lover beneath her opening her door to listen. Smilla
drops a piece of paper through the mail slot. Everyone waits.

MRS. SCHOU
You won't get away with anything. I can see you.
Elsa Lübing's door opens. She is formidable-
looking: six feet tall, wearing a long white dress,
gray hair pinned up, a silver cross at her throat. She
holds Juliane's pension letter in her hands.

LÜBING
I remember this letter quite well.

MRS. SCHOU
She said she had flowers!

LÜBING
It's all right, Mrs. Schou.
She steps aside and Smilla enters.

INT. ELSA LÜBING'S APARTMENT—
MORNING

An astounding view of Copenhagen. Almost nothing else in the apartment. A sofa, a table, two
chairs. A crucifix on the wall. Utter simplicity. She
and Smilla sit.

LÜBING
This time of day, I am normally at prayer.

She studies the letter again.
Norsaq Christiansen's death was a tragic accident, especially for the boy. A child needs both parents. That is one of the practical reasons marriage is sacred.

SMILLA
Mr. Lübing would be pleased to hear that.

LÜBING
There is no Mr. Lübing. I am the bride of Jesus.

SMILLA
The boy is dead. Four days ago he fell off a roof.
Elsa Lübing stands up, goes to the window.

LÜBING
I met him once. When I met him I knew why it was written that unless you become as children, you will not enter paradise. I hope his mother will find her way to Jesus.

SMILLA
Only if you can find Him at the bottom of a bottle.

LÜBING
He is everywhere—even there.

SMILLA
(Beat)
Someone chased the boy off the roof. He was murdered.

LÜBING
The Devil assumes many forms.

SMILLA
It's one of those forms that I'm looking for . . .
Do you know a Professor Loyen?

LÜBING
No.

SMILLA
Was he on the payroll of Greenland Mining?

LÜBING
I don't remember.

SMILLA
You said that you met Isaiah. When?

LÜBING
Greenland Mining began to hire Inuits for the geological expeditions. It was on one of these—an expedition in the summer of 1993 . . . on the Gela Alta glacier—that the father died. When we awarded the pension the boy and his mother came to my office.

SMILLA
How did the father die?

LÜBING
An explosion. You are interested in the past, Miss Jaspersen?

SMILLA
I'm interested in why the chief bookkeeper of Greenland Mining has such a guilty conscience she's writing notes in the margins of pension awards.
(Beat)
May I see the reports for that expedition?

LÜBING
They're in a safe in the archive department . . . There's nothing to see.

SMILLA
"Thou shalt not lie," Miss Lübing.

LÜBING
I think you should go now.
As Smilla turns to go:

LÜBING
Why do you think someone was chasing the little boy?

SMILLA
There was snow on the roof that he fell from. I saw his footprints. The way you have a sense of God—I have a sense of snow.
Elsa Lübing nods. Smilla is dismissed.

INT. ELSA LÜBING'S HALLWAY—DAY

Smilla, very disappointed, is leaving the building when the intercom suddenly crackles to life.

LÜBING (VOICE-OVER)
Miss Jaspersen . . .

SMILLA
Hello?

LÜBING (VOICE-OVER)
Would you come back up for a moment?

INT. ELSA LÜBING'S APARTMENT— DAY

Close-up Elsa Lübing as she opens the door to Smilla.

LÜBING
Just now, when you left, I opened it at the Book of Revelation. "And the fifth angel sounded, and I saw a star fall from heaven unto the earth: and to him was given the key of the bottomless pit."
Smilla says nothing. She is holding her breath . . .

LÜBING
The key to hell, Miss Jaspersen. How far will you go?

SMILLA
Try me.
Elsa Lübing regards her for a long moment, then:

(ABOVE) *Of course, the fierce dog was not poisoned but only anesthetized for a couple of minutes. Two veterinarians and the dog's owner were present throughout the shooting of the scene*

LÜBING
There are two archive sections in the basement of our building on Strand Boulevard. That's where the expedition reports are kept. Naturally, I cannot mention that there is a passkey system. Nor that the Abloy key on the wall behind you is for the main entrance to the building.
We see Smilla's hand in close-up as it reaches for the key and closes over it . . .

LÜBING
But someone has to guard the gates of hell . . .

EXT. STREET IN FRONT OF GREENLAND MINING—NIGHT

The deserted factory, behind a huge gate. Smilla is wearing thigh-high boots, a cap, a black jacket. She has a backpack on. The key does not fit the lock. Smilla curses, slings her backpack high over the wall, which she begins to climb.

EXT. GREENLAND MINING BUILDING—NIGHT

As Smilla drops to the ground we hear a terrible deep growl, as a horrible malevolent hound lunges for her throat.
Smilla holds up a piece of liver she's brought. It stops, swallows it in one bite. And then they stare at each other, the dog emitting a deep snarl, which starts to get weak, which turns into a whimper, which turns into a weak howl as its back legs give out. It tries to stand, to move forward, collapses on the ground, its tail thumping.

SMILLA
Good doggy. Good dog.
She steps over it and climbs the stairs to the building that houses the archives.

INT. ARCHIVE ROOMS—NIGHT

The first room is the entire basement area of one wing. Smilla enters the second room, filled with windows. She takes off her boots and goes to work, taping the windows with the huge sheets of plastic garbage bags. Then, using her flashlight, she begins to look for the expedition journals. She plays her flashlight over thick folders . . . "On the use of processed raw cryolite in the production of electric light bulbs." Smilla opens three or four of them and then finds the one she has been looking for:

The title page reads: "The geologic expedition of Greenland Mining to Gela Alta, July through August 1993." The folder is stuffed with other reports, X rays.

Smilla cannot resist taking the folder over to the far corner of the room and sitting down with it, leaning against a bookcase as she reads: ". . . to investigate the deposits of granular ruby crystals on the Barren Glacier on Gela Alta." Next, medical reports and X rays. As her eye travels down the page, Loyen's name—

Before Smilla can continue, a noise comes from the first archive room. Smilla turns off the flashlight. She sees a figure blocking the light from the doorway, and she stands up, goes behind an enormous bookshelf. As the figure enters the room, Smilla grabs the bookcase and topples it. As it picks up speed, books fly out, giving warning to the

figure. He tries to hold off the bookcase, but his legs finally slip out from under him and it crashes down on top of him. Smilla has grabbed a huge brass rod with maps hanging from it and slams the figure over the head. She drops it, picks up the flashlight, and shines it on . . . the Mechanic. Through the dust and blood she can see one ear has split. He's still conscious.

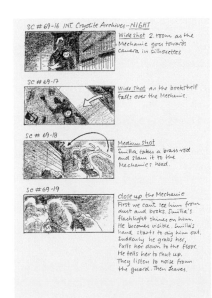

113

EXT. GREENLAND MINING BUILDING—NIGHT

They come out from the building. Smilla's arms are filled with heavy folders.

EXT. STREET IN FRONT OF GREENLAND MINING—NIGHT

They run to the Mechanic's old car.

INT. MECHANIC'S CAR—NIGHT

The Mechanic is driving the car through the dark streets. It has begun to snow.
   Silence between them. Then:

SMILLA
Why were you following me?

MECHANIC
I'd been thinking about what you said about the footprints. If you're right, you're in danger.
This scares her. She grows quiet.

INT. MECHANIC'S APARTMENT—NIGHT

Smilla enters with him, still carrying the reports she stole from Greenland Mining. He takes them from her and puts them down.
   She has never been here before. Wonderful blond-wood furniture covered with beautiful blankets. Candles and drawings. Roses in porcelain pots. Smilla is astounded, cannot reconcile this order and beauty with her image of him.
   He goes into the small, perfectly organized kitchen, begins to grind coffee beans. He puts them in a funnel, which he attaches to an espresso machine, and places this on a burner. He pours whipping cream and milk into two glasses. Smilla watches him, mesmerized.
   He froths the milk with the steam nozzle and pours the hot coffee into the glasses, hands her one. Begins to chop vegetables now.

MECHANIC
Isaiah and I were friends, you know. He used to m-m-make me laugh. He had this little game, you know, where he put his head in his hands like this and when he'd come up he would be a monkey or a rabbit or Frankenstein . . . or whatever . . . I-I used to see him come home sometimes in a cab, and he always seemed so . . . afraid.

SMILLA
They examined him every month. At the hospital. I think that's what scared him.

MECHANIC
Why? What do you think they were looking for?

SMILLA
I don't know. Someone also shoved a biopsy needle into him after he died. A very important doctor.
He puts the food on the table. They say nothing for

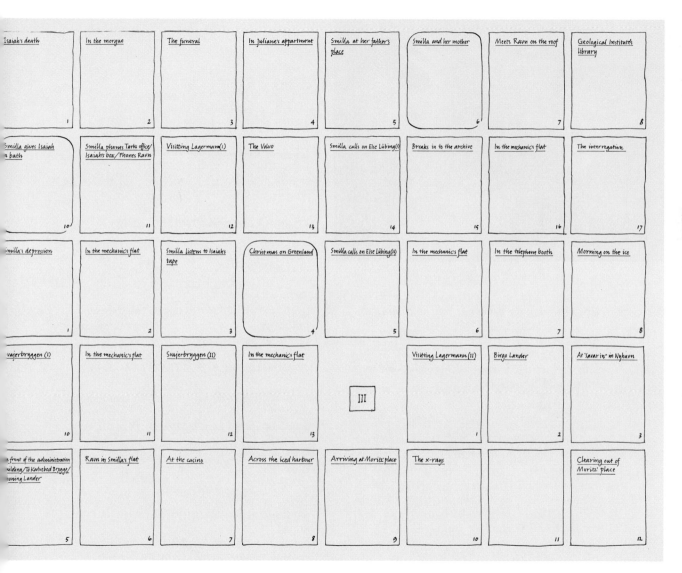

Isaiah's death	In the morgue	The funeral	In Juliane's appartment	Smilla at her father's place	Smilla and her mother	Meets Ravn on the roof	Geological Institute's library
1	2	3	4	5	6	7	8
Smilla gives Isaiah a bath	Smilla phones Torka office/ Isaiah's box/Phones Ravn	Visitting Lagermann (I)	The Volvo	Smilla calls on Else Lübing (I)	Breaks in to the archive	In the mechanic's flat	The interrogation
10	11	12	13	14	15	16	17
Smilla's depression	In the mechanic's flat	Smilla listens to Isaiah's tape	Christmas on Greenland	Smilla calls on Else Lübing (II)	In the mechanic's flat	In the telephone booth	Morning on the ice
1	2	3	4	5	6	7	8
Svajerbryggen (I)	In the mechanic's flat	Svajerbryggen (II)	In the mechanic's flat	III	Visitting Lagermann (II)	Birgo Lander	At "savarin" in Nyhavn
10	11	12	13		1	2	3
In front of the administration building/To Kalvebod Brygge/ phoning Lander	Ravn in Smilla's flat	At the casino	Across the iced harbour	Arriving at Moritz' place	The x-rays		Clearing out of Moritz' place
5	6	7	8	9	10	11	12

Before Bille August and Peter Høeg's meetings about the screenplay, the latter had made a clear outline of the novel's course of events

MECHANIC
Smilla, why does such a nice person have such a rough mouth?

SMILLA
I'm sorry I've given you the impression it's my mouth that's rough. I try to be rough all over.
He steps aside to let her go.

EXT. COPENHAGEN—NIGHT

The roofs and streets of nighttime Copenhagen are covered with snow.

INT. SMILLA'S APARTMENT—DAY

Smilla answers a ring at the door. Ravn and another man, COMBOVER, are standing outside.

RAVN
Miss Jaspersen? I'd like to talk to you, please?
Smilla doesn't open the door for them. Makes them linger in the hallway and steps outside.

INT. WHITE PALACE. STAIRWAY—DAY

Angle on the Mechanic, coming into the building, down below, outside his apartment. Walks to the stairwell and looks up, sees the backs of the men.

SMILLA
Talk.

RAVN
Would you be so kind as to follow us to the police station?
There is some veiled threat in his voice, Smilla knows this is not a request. She studies him for a moment.

a moment. Suddenly Smilla is uncomfortable with him, the food, the intimacy. She stands up.

SMILLA
(Stiffly)
I do appreciate it when someone makes me something good. Thank you.

MECHANIC
Don't go.
Smilla takes half the report and hands him half.

SMILLA
Isaiah's father was on an expedition for Greenland Mining when he died. That prick Loyen was the medical consultant. I saw his name in here. Try to read it. It will be good for your dyslexia.
She goes to the door. For a moment, the Mechanic blocks her way out.

SMILLA
No. I would not be so kind.

RAVN
I'm sorry. You must.
Taking an unspoken cue from Ravn, Combover grabs her and tries to pull her out before she can shut the door to her apartment. Smilla jerks away from him violently.

SMILLA
I'll come with you, just keep your hands off me. Keep your hands off me . . . Get your hands off me!
She begins to move—perhaps to go back in her apartment and get her things—when Combover is suddenly lifted off his feet. The Mechanic has pinned him up against the wall.
*   It is leverage rather than strength—he keeps one hand pressed against his windpipe.*

MECHANIC
I don't think you should g-g-go if you don't feel like it.
Ravn's hand moves to unbutton his jacket. The Mechanic looks at him, shakes his head no, presses harder on the windpipe. Ravn stops moving. Smilla looks at him.

SMILLA
Will I be driven home?

RAVN
To your door.

SMILLA
I can't resist a man with manners.
She studies him for a long moment, turns to the Mechanic.

SMILLA
I'll see you later.

The Mechanic lets him go. He slides down the wall, gasping for air. The Mechanic pats his hair back into place, then steps back to let them pass.

INT. POLICE HEADQUARTERS. HALLWAY—DAY

Smilla is brought along a hallway. A pathetic Christmas tree at the end of the corridor reminds us it is a holiday. Smilla is taken into a dark room with venetian blinds on the window.

INT. POLICE HEADQUARTERS. INTERROGATION ROOM—DAY

Ravn sits her down, turns on the light. A MAN is sitting on a chair in a corner. Close-cropped black hair, sinewy, distant blue eyes. Ravn opens a file and begins to read from it.

RAVN
Smilla Jaspersen. Born June 16, 1960, in Qaanaaq, Greenland. Parents: Ane Qaavigaaq Jaspersen, a

117

local hunter, and Moritz Jaspersen, American physician. In 1989 employed by the Geodetic Institute. From 1989 to '93 scientific participant in expeditions to the ice cap, the Arctic Ocean, and Arctic North America . . . Various references are attached. All of them state unanimously that if you want to know anything about ice, you would benefit by consulting Smilla Jaspersen.
(For the first time Ravn looks at the man in the background.)
Captain Telling here, however, has gathered some information of a different character.
Captain Telling comes over and hands Ravn a green file; he opens it.

RAVN
Moved to Denmark in 1967 after the death of your mother . . . Expelled from four boarding schools . . . Admitted to Copenhagen University, asked to leave a year later . . .
Then there are these other references, all of which state that you've created trouble wherever you've been. Arrested twice, once in Canada.

SMILLA
I was tagging polar bears. Bears don't read maps, so they don't respect national boundaries.

RAVN
(Ravn ignores her, continues.)
This paints a picture of a woman who has never completed a course of study. Who has been unemployed for years. Who has no family. Who has created conflict wherever she has been. Someone who has never been able to fit in.
(Beat)
Anyone with any sense would keep a very low profile in your position.

SMILLA
Is it my clothes you don't like?

RAVN
What we don't like is your fruitless and damaging attempts to meddle in the investigation of this case, which I have already promised you I would look into.

SMILLA
I remember what you promised me. Screw you, Ravn.
She gets up to leave. Another OFFICER, one we haven't seen before, enters the room and puts something down on the desk between Smilla and the men. It is the heavy folder and reports she stole from Greenland Mining. Smilla sits back down.

RAVN
These belong to Greenland Mining. We found them in your apartment . . .
For the first time, Captain Telling speaks.

TELLING
Imprisonment in a little soundproof room with no windows is, I've been told, particularly difficult if you've been brought up in Greenland.
Smilla looks at him. There is some deep negotiation going on now. Smilla holds her breath . . .

TELLING
This would cause you extreme distress?
Smilla says nothing. The fight has visibly gone out of her.

TELLING
It's true, is it not?
Smilla finally manages a nod.

TELLING
They say it's something about the vast spaces. The horizon.
(Beat)
Is that what it is—all that space?
He waits. She nods again.

TELLING
Good. Then we mustn't let that happen. We've reached an agreement, then?

SMILLA
(Very quietly)
Yes.

TELLING
Will you say this louder, please. So I can hear you.

SMILLA
(Totally humiliated)
Yes. We've reached an agreement.

RAVN
You may go now.
Smilla waits quietly, her head bowed in supplication and shame.

INT. SMILLA'S APARTMENT— EVENING

Smilla enters in the dark. From where she is standing, without the energy to move, her eye falls on different objects, picks out the subtle disarray: her place has been thoroughly searched. We can see the shattering sense of violation she feels.

INT. SMILLA'S APARTMENT— EVENING

Smilla is sitting in a chair. She is not reading, she is not eating, she is not listening to music. She is utterly and completely defeated. Her hair is dirty, she looks as if she hasn't slept. The doorbell rings. She ignores it.

INT. WHITE PALACE. STAIRWAY—EVENING

The Mechanic continues to ring her bell. He looks worried.

INT. SMILLA'S APARTMENT—EVENING

Smilla finally drags herself to her feet and goes to answer the door. Instead, she stops in front of the door where the ringing apparatus is and silences it with a screwdriver.

DISSOLVE TO:
INT. SMILLA'S APARTMENT—EVENING

Smilla lies on the sofa.

EXT. GREENLAND—DAY (FLASHBACK)

Around a fire, six-year-old Smilla, her mother, and the other hunters, all men, sit feasting on a raw seal, which they have just shot. Her mother is beautiful: deep-brown burnished skin, her hair pulled back in a bun, wearing bearskin pants. She lifts up her ano-

rak and pulls Smilla to her, between her legs, and Smilla drinks from her full breast.

INT. SMILLA'S APARTMENT—EVENING

Smilla is still lying on her sofa. Her phone rings. Her machine picks up. After her announcement and the beep:

MORITZ
This is your father. Could you come for lunch tomorrow at the club? Call me back, please—
Smilla goes and rips out the cord to the answering machine as well, cutting him off in mid-sentence. Smilla takes her seat again.
This time, a huge piece of cardboard is slipped under her door, onto the floor.

INT. MECHANIC'S APARTMENT— EVENING

Wearing his reading glasses, he is reading the files from Greenland Mining that Smilla left with him. Three X rays lie on the table. Smilla opens his door and walks in, without knocking. She is holding the piece of cardboard. Reads it.

SMILLA
"Anything is better than suicide."
(Beat)
How can you have six spelling mistakes in five words?
She tosses it on his table. She looks better, has combed her hair.

SMILLA
I'm not suicidal. Suicide is for cowards.
He sits up, takes off his glasses.

SMILLA
Sometimes one just wants to be left alone, that's all.

She can't sit down, can't stand still suddenly. She paces around, in a state of extreme agitation. He gestures toward the report he's been reading.

MECHANIC
There was an earlier expedition—in 1966. There was an accident that time, too. Two of the eight men died. Loyen was on both expeditions.

SMILLA
I can't be part of this.
I came to tell you that. I'm out of it. Good luck.
He studies her for a long moment.

MECHANIC
Smilla . . . What did they d-d-do to you?
Beat.

SMILLA
They threatened to lock me up. I can't be locked up.
He still doesn't say anything.

SMILLA
I'm quite ashamed. Really I am. I just can't be locked up.
He gets up, moves toward her. Looks for a moment as if he's going to put his arms around her. She puts her arms up to ward it off.

SMILLA
Don't.

MECHANIC
It's okay, Smilla.

SMILLA
Do you think I need you to understand me?
A long beat.
Dead silence. Smilla has even shocked herself this time.

SMILLA
I'm sorry. What is it about you that makes me want
to insult you?

**INT. MECHANIC'S APARTMENT. KITCHEN—
EVENING**

*The Mechanic has cooked dinner for them. They sit
eating.*

SMILLA
When my father first brought me here from Greenland I refused to sleep indoors. I couldn't stand it,
the heat. I was used to the snow, the air. I made a
tent on our lawn. Poor Moritz, he was so embar-
rassed. Even now, my idea of hell is to be locked up.

MECHANIC
Wh-where was your mother?

SMILLA
She went out one day to hunt. They found her kayak a few days later. The side had been staved in. No
one who falls into the water in Greenland ever
comes up again. The sea is less than thirty-nine degrees Fahrenheit, and at that temperature all the
processes of decomposition stop.

MECHANIC
How old were you?

SMILLA
Six.

MECHANIC
That's when you came here?

SMILLA
That's when my father brought me here.

MECHANIC
But you were never happy here?

SMILLA
The only thing that makes me truly happy is
mathematics . . . Snow, ice, and numbers . . .
The Mechanic eats, listening.

SMILLA
The number system is like human life. First you
have the natural numbers. The ones that are whole
and positive. Like the numbers of a small child. But
human consciousness expands. The child discovers
longing. Do you know the mathematical expression
for longing?
The Mechanic still eats, shakes his head.

SMILLA
The negative numbers. The formalization of the
feeling that you're missing something. And then the

121

fore she can, he pours two glasses of champagne, comes close to her, hands her one.

MECHANIC
Smilla, it's Christmas Eve. Toast with me.

SMILLA
To what?

MECHANIC
To Isaiah.
She puts the glass down.

SMILLA
Don't you understand? My heart is broken.

MECHANIC
Then to a merry Christmas and a happy New Year.
She shakes her head—he couldn't possibly be this stupid. Then walks out of the apartment. He stands watching her, puts his glass down.

INT. WHITE PALACE. STAIRWELL—EVENING

As Smilla takes the stairs up to her apartment, she hears Juliane on the stair above her.

JULIANE
Smilla . . .
Smilla takes the stairs up a flight, is met by a shocking sight: Juliane is clean, has fresh clothes on . . . is sober.

SMILLA
You look wonderful.

JULIANE
Two days, Smilla. No drinking.
She holds out her hands, Smilla takes them. Juliane laughs with embarrassment.

child discovers the in-between spaces—between stones, between people, between numbers—and that produces fractions. But it doesn't stop there . . .
(Takes another bite.)
. . . because between any two fractions there's an infinite number of irrational numbers like pi that can never be written down. They force human consciousness out beyond its limits. But it's a kind of madness, because it doesn't even stop there. It never stops. There are numbers we can't even begin to comprehend . . .
The Mechanic observes her closely.

SMILLA
Mathematics is a vast, open landscape. You head toward the horizons, but they always keep receding—like happiness—like Greenland. That's what I can't live without—that's why I can't be locked up.

MECHANIC
Smilla, can I kiss you?
She is astounded by this request. Cannot look at him, looks at her plate. Then stands up to go. Be-

JULIANE
I have something for you.
She goes inside. Smilla follows her in.

**INT. JULIANE'S APARTMENT—
EVENING**

Juliane hands Smilla a small cigar box.

JULIANE
Merry Christmas, Smilla. He hid this box good.
You should keep it now. Open it.
*Smilla opens it. It is filled with Isaiah's most trea-
sured objects. She is very moved to see these things
again: A special knife she gave him. An ancient harpoon head. A picture of him with his father. His
passport. A small length of rope with a suction cup
attached to it. An odd toy. And a battered Walkman. Smilla takes it out.*

SMILLA
His Walkman . . .

JULIANE
You gave it to him last Christmas, remember. It was
his best present.
*Smilla nods, takes up the snapshot of Isaiah and his
father. The sun is in their eyes. They are in Greenland, standing by an ice-drilling structure with the
Greenland Mining logo on the side of it. Both are
stripped to the waist, grinning into the camera.*

SMILLA
They let Isaiah go with them on the expedition?

JULIANE
The Greenland Mining people were looking for
men in Greenland. My husband signed on. They
told us that Isaiah could go with him, so how dangerous could it be? They were digging inside a
glacier. Something must have happened . . . Isaiah

was outside. They took his dad in a helicopter to
the hospital, and there his dad died. He never saw
him again.

SMILLA
What really happened, Juliane?

JULIANE
Be careful, Smilla. It was not an accident. There
was something in the meltwater. Isaiah told me so.

SMILLA
In the meltwater? How would Isaiah know?

JULIANE
His daddy told him.
Smilla looks totally confused.

SMILLA
But he couldn't have done . . .
*Juliane looks nervous, as though wishing she had
never started.*

SMILLA
You just said they flew your husband away in a
helicopter . . .

JULIANE
Smilla, please. No more questions.
There is a look of real fear in Juliane's eyes.

SMILLA
Who brought Isaiah home?

JULIANE
This doctor. Loyen.

SMILLA
Was Isaiah sick, Juliane? Is that why Loyen examined him every month?

JULIANE
Smilla, please, no more questions . . .

**INT. WHITE PALACE. STAIRWAY—
NIGHT**

*Smilla goes down to the Mechanic's apartment and
knocks on the door. He opens it.*

SMILLA
I'm scared, but I'll do it anyway.

MECHANIC
I knew you would.
*He goes to get the glasses, comes back, and hands
one to her.*

SMILLA
The Inuits believe that if you kill something, you
offend its soul. I need his soul to be at peace.
*He raises his glass, they touch glasses. They are
about to drink. Smilla lowers her glass.*

SMILLA
Did you ever hear the phrase "she was so drunk she
didn't know what she was doing"?
He nods.

SMILLA
That's why I'm doing this before I drink anything.
*And she kisses him. He leans down to kiss her,
stunned by the arrival of the longed-for thing. She
takes his hands, puts them around her. He pushes
her back against the banister. The kiss goes on, until
Smilla breaks away. Without another word, she
disappears up the stairs to her apartment. The
Mechanic stands there, waits, then calls out to her.*

SMILLA
Go back inside . . .

Bille August goes through the scene in Moritz's club with Julia Ormond, Robert Loggia (Moritz), and Emma Croft (Benja), just before the shoot

MECHANIC
Smilla?
She leans out over the stairway—smiles . . .

SMILLA
What?

MECHANIC
(Dead serious)
Don't answer the phone from now on.
Smilla stares at him a moment, goes into the apartment and closes the door, terrified again.

EXT. CLUB—DAY

Fancy cars drive up and disgorge well-dressed couples and families. We see Smilla moving toward the entrance.

INT. CLUB—DAY

A private club for the elite of Copenhagen. Members only, elegant and clubby. Roaring fireplaces, Biedermeier and crystal, good paintings, excellent food on this freezing Christmas Day . . . Smilla's father, Moritz, and Benja are about to eat when Smilla walks in. His face lights up when he sees her.

MORITZ
What a surprise! We were not expecting you.

BENJA
(Sour)
I thought you didn't celebrate Christmas.

SMILLA
I don't.

BENJA
So what *do* you celebrate, Smilla?

SMILLA
I celebrate the loners, the outcasts, the shy girl with
pimples, the fattest boy in class, the dyslexics, the
stutterers, the premature ejaculators.
Smilla smiles at Benja.

BENJA
You're such a freak.
Smilla opens up her backpack, pulls out the medical

*records and X rays from the Greenland Mining
expedition.*

SMILLA
Some men died on an expedition to the west coast
of Greenland. I need to know why. Will you look at
these for me?

MORITZ
I thought you wanted to have lunch with us.

SMILLA
Do this for me, Moritz. I'm happy today for the
first time in ages.
*He nods, sweeps them up, and puts them away.
Studies her.*
   *Smilla looks past him, suddenly sees the sleek
white head of the man from the funeral whom
Juliane spit on. He is huddled with some men; they
are lighting cigars. The others have their backs
turned to Smilla.*

SMILLA
The man with the white hair—do you know him?

MORITZ
Dr. Andreas Tørk, head of Greenland Mining. He's
a specialist in Arctic mineralogy. Very ambitious
and powerful. Why? Do you want to meet him?

SMILLA
Why would someone examine a child every month
at a hospital?

MORITZ
If he'd been exposed to a virus . . .

SMILLA
Why would someone shove a biopsy needle into a
dead six-year-old?

BENJA
Oh, gross. I'm not eating now. Forget it.

SMILLA
(Can't stop looking at Tørk.)
Answer me.

BENJA
I'm not eating a bloody thing now, Moritz.

MORITZ
(Weary, upset)
I don't know, Smilla.
(Beat)
To measure the progress of something.
Smilla gets up and kisses him, never taking her eyes off Andreas Tørk.

SMILLA
Thank you, Father. Call me when you've looked at them.
> *She grabs her backpack, leaves the room.*
> *Smilla's point of view as she moves toward the smoking room where Tørk is. As she comes closer, a man comes into view from behind a couch. It is the Mechanic.*
> *Smilla's face as she registers this shock. The Mechanic sees her, his face betrays nothing, he continues to talk.*
> *Smilla turns around and starts out of the club.*

EXT. CLUB—DAY

Smilla has made it outside, is hurrying down toward a road thick with cars. The Mechanic catches up with her. She is rigid with anger, tries to pull away from him.

MECHANIC
I was following you, he recognized me from the funeral. He stopped me and asked me how Juliane was doing. That's all.

SMILLA
You were *with* him.

MECHANIC
I wasn't with him. We started to talk. I thought I could learn more about Greenland Mining. I was following you there—
Smilla almost runs down the street.

MECHANIC
Smilla . . . Smilla, don't you trust me?
She searches his face, wants to believe him. Looks as if she does, but then times it so a truck is hurtling toward them on the road.

SMILLA
No.
And makes a run for it, just as the truck is bearing down. She beats it across the road by seconds. The

Mechanic is stuck on the other side. When the traffic finally lets up, she is gone.

INT. SMILLA'S APARTMENT—DUSK

Smilla sits with Isaiah's cigar box. She pulls out the rope with the suction cups attached, turns it over in her hands. It is a strange apparatus, she tries to figure out what kind of toy it is, and . . .

INT. WHITE PALACE. STAIRWAY—EVENING (FLASHBACK)

Isaiah sits crying under the stairs with his knife and the suction cups.
   Smilla comes out into the stairwell because she has heard noise coming from downstairs. Juliane's door below is open and the voices are distinct now. Smilla sees two men come out with a clearly intoxicated Juliane staggering after them, shouting.

JULIANE
I told you . . . we have nothing . . . nothing, you fucking bastards . . .
Suddenly one of the men, Verlaine, turns around and slaps Juliane's face. She breaks down and yells at the two men, who disappear down the stairs.

JULIANE
Leave us alone!
She walks back into her apartment, slams the door violently. The men are gone and the stairwell suddenly becomes completely silent. Then Smilla hears a child crying quietly under the stairs at the bottom of the stairwell.

INT. WHITE PALACE. BOTTOM OF STAIRWAY—EVENING (FLASHBACK CONT.)

Smilla finds Isaiah sitting hunched up under the stairs to the basement.

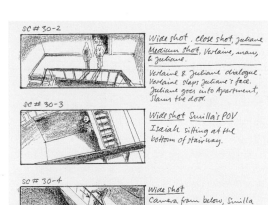

SC # 30-2

Wide shot . close shot, Juliane
Medium shot, Verlaine, men,
& Juliane.

Verlaine & Juliane dialogue.
Verlaine slaps Juliane's face.
Juliane goes into Apartment,
slams the door.

SC # 30-3

Wide shot Smilla's POV
Isaiah sitting at the
bottom of stairway.

SC # 30-4

Wide shot
Camera from below, Smilla
runs down stairway.
She kneels down next to
Isaiah.

SMILLA
What's happened?
He is trembling with fear, his entire body shivers,
she cannot get in contact with him. She bends down
and puts her arms around him.

SMILLA
It's okay . . . It's me, Smilla . . .
(Strokes his tearful face with her hand.)
Isaiah.
Only now she sees that he is holding a knife and
two small strange toy suction cups attached to
either end of a piece of string.

INT. SMILLA'S APARTMENT—DUSK

We are back with Smilla playing with Isaiah's suc-
tion cups. She presses one against a piece of Green-
landic rock on her table, pulls the string—the stone
moves. Something occurs to Smilla.

INT. WHITE PALACE. STAIRWAY— DUSK

Smilla arrives at the bottom landing. She gets to her
knees, looks into the crawl space. It is small, next to
an electrical box. Smilla gets on her back and slides
in, holding the suction cups.
    Her point of view: The ceiling is bricked in.
When her eyes adjust to the dim light, she notices
that one brick is different from the others—it has
white mortar around the edges. Smilla takes the
suction cups and attaches them. Nothing. Does it
again, this time working it, pulling at it. Little by
little it begins to give. Smilla is sweating. Keeps at
it, gains purchase on it. Wedges one edge out and
keeps at it, wets a cup with a finger, attaches it
again. This time the brick gives—mortar falls onto
her face and hair. She sticks her hand in, feels
around, when she hears the Mechanic come into the
building. He is a few feet from her. Her heart is

pounding, thinking he can hear her. She waits,
hears him climb the stairs to her apartment.

MECHANIC'S VOICE
Smilla?
Then she hears him come back down. It is only
when he shuts his door that she sticks her hand
back into the hiding place . . . searches around, and
her hand closes over something. She pulls it out: it
is an old, dusty, ordinary audiocassette tape.

INT. SMILLA'S APARTMENT—DUSK

She pops the cassette into Isaiah's player. The sound
is awful, she can barely hear anything—just a series
of scrambled sounds . . . bits of Greenlandic, but
the effect is eerie and terrifying.

EXT. SOUTH HARBOR—DAY

Smilla walks through this industrial ghost town.
The sky is low and gray, filled with coal smoke and
chemicals from the factories. Snow is banked on
either side of the roads.
    No signs of life except for an occasional diesel
truck passing through the streets. A cafeteria adver-
tises sausages.

Suddenly this dismal view opens onto a picture postcard scene: a huge harbor basin surrounded by warehouses. Smilla makes her way to the South Wharf, where an ancient three-masted sailing ship is docked.

Angle on Smilla as she walks down the gangway to the ship. A sign tells us this is the ARCTIC MUSEUM.

Angle on a Range Rover, hidden by the side of one of the warehouses. We can barely make out two men inside, who are obscured by the tinted glass. They watch Smilla as she enters the ship.

INT. ARCTIC MUSEUM—DAY

Smilla makes her way downstairs. She enters a huge, dimly lit room. A man is sitting behind a desk: much older than Smilla, vaguely Inuit-looking. He is surrounded by sound equipment of every kind, mixed in with Inuit and military artifacts. This is LICHT.

LICHT
How did you find me?

SMILLA
It wasn't hard. You're considered the best ear in Copenhagen.

LICHT
You called about a tape?
She hands him the tape, which has been in her backpack. Licht turns his back to her, works at a console filled with very sophisticated sound equipment. Smilla hears the same muffled sound she heard when she played it the first time.

SMILLA
It was left next to an electrical box. Maybe that's what affected the sound on it. I can't make it out . . .
Licht has been twiddling knobs, setting levels, etc.

He plays the tape: still the same muffled sound. Licht alters settings, manages to filter out a little surface noise.

LICHT
Sounds like some kind of announcement . . .
We can hear no better than Smilla can.

SMILLA
I can't hear anything.

LICHT
That's because you haven't trained your ear.
He replays the tape, and this time we can just make out a voice, which sounds somehow mechanical.

LICHT
Hear it now? It's not live—it's coming from a loud-speaker . . .
(Beat)
. . . an intercom. Maybe in a hospital somewhere—can you hear the doctor's beeper?

SMILLA
(Astonished)
No.
Licht rewinds the tape, resets the EQ filters.

LICHT
(Plays tape again.)
There's someone whispering, too . . . He's in a lot of pain . . . There's an EEG in there as well, monitoring his heart . . . Hear it now?
Again Smilla shakes her head, utterly astonished at his perception. Licht is delighted.

SMILLA
What's he saying?

LICHT
I can't tell, I'm afraid—it's in dialect. I can speak a

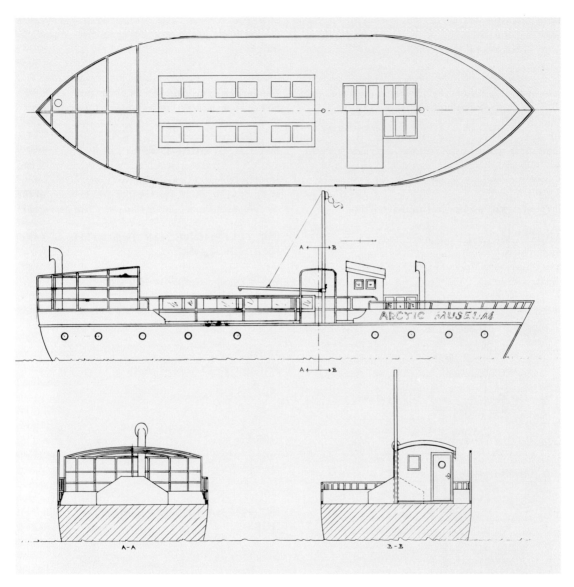

Production designer Anna Asp's idea of the ship that houses the Arctic Museum. Drawing by Love Malmsten

little East Greenlandic, but this is from the Northwest, around Thule, I'd say—yes . . . Did you hear that? A Sikorsky R17 overhead . . . Late '93, early '94?

We can faintly verify the sounds that Licht identifies—but only because he's telling us first. He smiles at her, very proud of himself.

LICHT
This must be the hospital in the American Air Base in Thule.

SMILLA
Is there any way you can clean up the tape?

LICHT
Come back in an hour.
She is fascinated by him, reluctant to go . . .

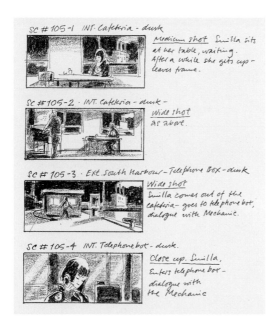

SMILLA
I'm amazed you can conclude so much from so little.

LICHT
Blindness sharpens the sense of hearing.
Smilla looks at him and realizes for the first time that he is blind.

INT. CAFETERIA—DUSK

It is already dark out. Smilla sits alone, being stared at by a few workers, the smell of grease heavy in the air. She puts down her cup of watery tea, gets up.

INT. TELEPHONE BOOTH. SOUTH HARBOR—DUSK

Smilla goes to a phone booth, dials a number.

MECHANIC'S VOICE
Hello.

SMILLA
Were you really just following me?

MECHANIC'S VOICE
Yes.

SMILLA
I want to kiss you again.
(Long beat)
Would you like that?

INT. MECHANIC'S APARTMENT—DUSK

MECHANIC
(On the phone with Smilla)
Yes.

(Beat)
Smilla, where are you?
In the background, we can hear the sound of a fog-horn.

INT. TELEPHONE BOOTH. SOUTH HARBOR—DUSK

MECHANIC'S VOICE
Smilla . . .
She hangs up.

EXT. ARCTIC MUSEUM—NIGHT

It has turned dark now, as Smilla makes her way down the gangway and into the ship.

INT. ARCTIC MUSEUM—NIGHT

Smilla comes down the stairs. It is darker than before. She stops, scared to go farther. It is much too dark and quiet.

SMILLA
Mr. Licht?
Her eyes adjust to the light. She feels her way. Suddenly the light from the decks above illuminates Licht, who sits absolutely motionless in his chair.

She moves deeper into the room. Licht still doesn't move. It is only when she is next to him that she sees he is dead. She remains calm, reaches quickly for the pulse in his neck. There is none. Removes the headphones from his ears, and blood pours from them. At that moment, Smilla hears the door closing shut above her.

Smilla hears the engine of the ship start up, feels it start to move away from the dock.

She runs to the door at the top of the stairs. It is closed. She tries to push it open, but it is locked.

SMILLA
(Shouts.)
Open the door! Open the door!
Smilla comes back down again as the first explosion hits.

This is just a warmup to the explosion now, as the diesel engine goes. Smilla is thrown across the room as the wall blows off.

INT. RANGE ROVER. SOUTH HARBOR. DOCK—NIGHT

Verlaine and another man watch the exploding boat. Then they drive off.

INT. ARCTIC MUSEUM—NIGHT

Smilla is staring out into the ocean, the dock hundreds of feet away, the ship sailing directly toward a solid wall of fire where the engine landed and the chemicals are on fire.

As the boat begins to sink and list, Licht comes rolling into her, tied to his desk chair. She pushes him aside, and he slams into the bulkhead and then goes straight into the ocean.

Smilla is standing in water up to her knees now. She takes off her heavy coat . . . takes a huge breath, and dives off the boat, into the freezing water.

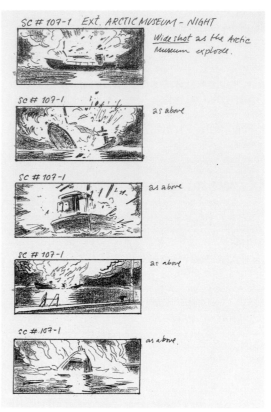

(ABOVE) Here are Simon Bang's drawings of the various camera angles that Bille August wanted to film the exploding ship from—an excellent aid for the special-effects people and others of the crew

134

EXT. WATER—NIGHT

One last huge explosion on board as Smilla swims back toward the dock. She begins to shake as her temperature drops. Her arms grow tired. She knows enough about water and freezing to death to know she is dead in another few seconds in the water. As she starts to approach the dock, her arms flailing, she can barely lift them. She stops, floats for a moment, can go no farther.

Summoning a last effort, Smilla manages to reach the dock and haul herself up.

EXT. SOUTH HARBOR. DOCK—NIGHT

A car pulls up and bright headlights illuminate the water.

EXT. SOUTH HARBOR. DOCK—NIGHT

The Mechanic pulls Smilla to her feet and half carries her to the car. She is hallucinating, her bare feet dragging in the snow, until he lifts her up and puts her in the car, covering her with his coat. He gets in and they drive off.

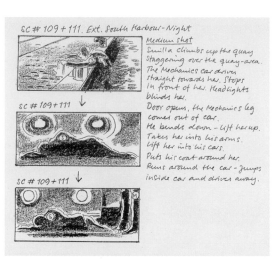

SC # 109 + 111. Ext. South Harbour - Night

<u>Medium shot</u>
Smilla climbs up the quay
staggering over the quay-area.
The Mechanics car drives
straight towards her. Stops
in front of her. Headlights
blinds her.

SC # 109 + 111 ↓

Door opens, the Mechanics leg
comes out of car.
He bends down - Lift her up.
Takes her into his arms.
Lift her into his cars.
Puts his coat around her.
Runs around the car - jumps
inside car and drives away.

SC # 109 + 111 ↓

INT. MECHANIC'S CAR—NIGHT

Smilla is smiling, drifting into unconsciousness—
He grabs her face . . .

MECHANIC
Talk to me . . . You have to talk now, Smilla . . .
Snow—talk to me about snow . . .

SMILLA
So many. There's too many kinds . . .

MECHANIC
Say them.

SMILLA
Qanik.

MECHANIC
What's that? *Talk!*

SMILLA
Falling snow.

MECHANIC
What other kinds?

SMILLA
Aqilluqqag. Wet snow, but not firm enough to build
a snow house with.
(Fierce)
You must never use it for that.

MECHANIC
I won't.

SMILLA
Promise me.

MECHANIC
I promise. More . . . Come on, more . . .

136

And as he holds her face and forces her to remember . . .

INT. MECHANIC'S APARTMENT. BEDROOM—NIGHT

He is sitting her down on the bed, tries to cover her. She is in excruciating agony now as her temperature returns to normal. She is on fire, weeping, in a state of hallucinatory pain. She cannot shut up . . . as if her talking will ward off the demons.

SMILLA
Did you get the tape? They killed Isaiah for it. Did you get it?

MECHANIC
No.

SMILLA
He could have made it. Not like Smilla the fake. The fake Greenlander with her fine clothes and her manners. I let him die.

MECHANIC
No you didn't.
She is sobbing now.

MECHANIC
The tablets will start to work in a few minutes. Then it won't hurt so much. You must sleep now.
He lays her down on the bed. She whispers to him urgently.

SMILLA
When I was little I knew where I was going.

MECHANIC
Yes.

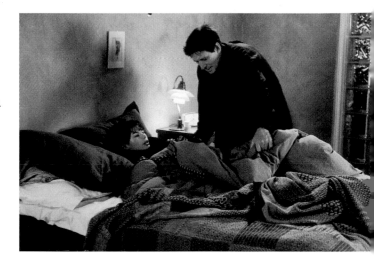

SMILLA
I'm very lost now.
She closes her eyes as he wipes her forehead. Her hand has a bandage on it. She finally falls asleep, holding on to one of his large hands.

EXT. COPENHAGEN—NIGHT

INT. MECHANIC'S APARTMENT. BEDROOM—NIGHT

Smilla as she sits bolt upright in bed. The Mechanic has been sitting in a chair, monitoring her condition. He sees the look of absolute terror on her face, is at her side. He calms her down, lays her back on the pillows. She won't let go of him, her eyes wide in terror, still lost in her dreams.

SMILLA
Stay with me.

MECHANIC
I'm right here.

SMILLA
Lie down with me.
*He does, his arms go around her, the weight of him
behind her reassuring her back into sleep.*

DISSOLVE TO:
INT. MECHANIC'S APARTMENT.
BEDROOM—DAWN

*The room is suffused with pale morning light. Smilla
wakes up. She watches the Mechanic, starts to
touch him, puts her leg across him. They begin to
make love very tenderly.*

CUT TO:
INT. MECHANIC'S APARTMENT.
BEDROOM—MORNING

*The weak, early morning winter sun shines into the
room. Smilla and the Mechanic are lying close
together in the bed.*

SMILLA
Kinngusaqattaarpoq.

MECHANIC
What does it mean?

SMILLA
Say it.

MECHANIC
I can't say it.

SMILLA
(Laughs.)
To practice rolling over in a kayak.

(Another now, faster)
Makittaqanngitsoq—

MECHANIC
Jesus—

SMILLA
—someone who has never mastered the art of rolling over in a kayak.
And finally . . .

SMILLA
Umiiarneq. A shipwrecked person.
*Her eyes fill with tears. His hand comes up to
smooth the hair away from her face.*

MECHANIC
You're not shipwrecked.
She takes his hand. Says one last word in Inuit:

SMILLA
Pilluaqaanga.
(A beat; translates.)
. . . to be deeply happy.
*A beat. Suddenly Smilla becomes very aware of the
intimacy. She feels awkward and sits up in bed
abruptly. Starts to get dressed.*
     She gets up to leave.

MECHANIC
Smilla?
When she turns back to look at him . . .

MECHANIC
Listen to me: you can't stay in your apartment.
They tried to kill you once, and if they find out
you're alive they won't make the same mistake
again. Go to your father's house. You'll be safer
with him.

INT. MECHANIC'S CAR—NIGHT

Smilla and the Mechanic drive in silence. He is distracted, studies the rearview mirror.

MECHANIC
We're being followed.
Smilla turns her head to look at him.

He speeds up, begins to push the small car through a punishing series of turns.

EXT. COPENHAGEN STREETS— NIGHT

The car behind them, the Range Rover we saw earlier, keeps up with them.

The Mechanic has approached a long pedestrians—only street, the Strøget, slamming down a side street toward this densely packed strip that intersects the city for miles.

The Range Rover keeps pace with them, turning now onto the side street.

The Mechanic keeps on, the crowd of shoppers turning at the sound of the car bearing down on them. As they part, the Mechanic whips the car into a turn, going against the thick crowd of pedestrians. Off the pedestrian street now, down another side street, and then back on, in a dizzying series of turns.

The Mechanic turns quickly onto a side street, stops, and waits for the Range Rover to drive past. Then backs out again, pulling out into traffic.

EXT. COPENHAGEN STREET— NIGHT

They are now following the Range Rover. Traffic is still thick, allowing them this subterfuge.

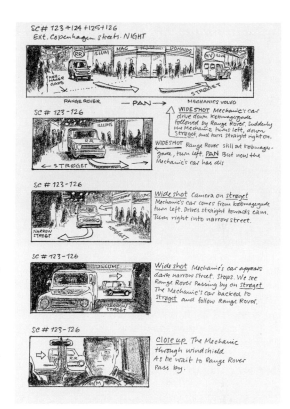

EXT. DOCKS—NIGHT

They have followed the Range Rover to the docks, travel behind it at a safe distance. It pulls up to something they cannot see yet because of the thick fog near the water.

As they come closer, it looms up out of the night, an enormous four-thousand-ton cargo ship. The name on the side tells us it is:

The Kronos. As hundreds of workers service this gray monster—cranes strain to lift cargo onto the open upper deck, arc welders weld, everything is lit

MECHANIC
There has got to be something else on that tape . . .
like what they really found up there in Greenland.
(Beat)
They're planning to go up again.
(He looks at Smilla.)

SMILLA
They've had to wait till now, when the pack ice
melts in Davis Strait . . .
They do not say anything for a moment.

MECHANIC
I know a man who knows about boats.

INT. MORITZ'S HOUSE. OFFICE—NIGHT

*Moritz sits with the X rays and reports Smilla gave
him in the club. He talks to Smilla. Benja sits in a
chair, playing with a scarf. We are in Moritz's
private examination room, an elegant marvel of
modern medical technology. Moritz reads from the
reports.*

MORITZ
Norsaq Christiansen, dead on the Gela Alta glacier,
July 1993. It says in a report that he died in an
explosion.
(Beat)
But I don't think that's what killed these people . . .
*Moritz hangs an X ray up on a light box. It shows
the inner organs of a human body.*

MORITZ
These are enlargements I made from the negatives.
You can see what remains of the liver, the lower
esophagus, and the stomach. This is the heart.
What's left of it. Smilla, do you notice something
unusual here?
He turns to Smilla.

up—it is like a huge city being readied for some
enormous undertaking.
   *The Mechanic has pulled the car behind a
warehouse. They watch undetected.*
   *They see two men supervising the activities: it's
Tørk and Verlaine.*

INT. MECHANIC'S CAR—NIGHT

The Mechanic and Smilla watch them.

MECHANIC
They found something in '66. Something went
wrong and they wait almost thirty years to send
another expedition. This time something else went
wrong. There was an accident. Four men died . . .
One of them was Isaiah's father.

SMILLA
So before Isaiah's father dies he sends his son a tape
telling him what really happened. Tørk comes looking for the tape. They kill Isaiah to get it. And then
they kill the man at the Arctic Museum.

SMILLA
Something's got into the heart. But what is it?

A needle-thin, whitish line, uneven, wanders up along the smashed vertebrae, disappears at the ribs, reappears at the tip of one lung, vanishes, and shows up again near the heart, outside and partly inside of it, in the large ventricle, like a white thread of light. Moritz picks up a scientific journal he's brought, Nature, *and hands it to Smilla, open to a particular page. An X ray, with a similar pattern of white light running through the bones and organs.*

BENJA
This is gross. What's it got to do with us?
Smilla looks up at her. And then she looks at Moritz and can barely snarl out the words.

SMILLA
Get her out of here.
Moritz turns and stands up to Benja for the first time.

MORITZ
Darling, please wait for me outside, I'll join you later? All right?

BENJA
But it's disgusting. What does it have to do with us?

MORITZ
I'll be with you soon . . . Please . . . please . . .
Moritz turns her around and gives her a little push toward the door.
    Moritz turns back and hangs up two more X rays, also showing inner organs, but more horrible.

MORITZ
Smilla, it is the arctic worm. *Dracunculus borealis.* Prehistoric. No one has ever seen pictures of them before. Loyen must have taken them.

SMILLA
But I thought the worm was extinct.

MORITZ
I thought so, too, Smilla. The question is what brought it back to life . . .
He hangs up a picture of the pregnant worm, its uterus tightly packed with larvae. He points at the last two X rays.

MORITZ
You see: the female worm entered these men's vital organs—the uterus bursts—there are ten million larvae released. The men go into toxic shock and they die on the spot. But it's very strange . . . parasites don't usually kill their hosts. It's very bad manners.
Smilla is horrified.

INT. MORITZ'S HOUSE. LIBRARY—NIGHT

Many hours later. Smilla can't sleep. She's in Moritz's library, studying Loyen's book on parasites.

Moritz wanders in, pours himself a shot of brandy, hands one to Smilla. Tonight, she drinks it.

MORITZ
Why are you getting involved in this?

SMILLA
I told you before, a child died. It's my New Year's resolution to make someone pay.

MORITZ
And this friend who dropped you off, he's also involved?
A long beat.

SMILLA
I don't know. I don't know him very well.
(Beat)
He has a repair shop which he never goes to. His hands are much too clean. He lies to me. I don't know what he does.
Moritz studies her for a moment.

MORITZ
Are you in love with him?

SMILLA
I've been trying to avoid it all my life, so now it's here I just want to renounce it.
Moritz sits across from her, studies his difficult daughter.

MORITZ
I'm sorry to hear that.

SMILLA
I'm tired. I'm tired of wondering why it is that every day I'm on this earth I'm in exile.

MORITZ
I'm sorry you're so angry. I'm sorry I made you do things . . .

SMILLA
Is it time for confession, Moritz? What things did you make me do?

MORITZ
I made you leave your country . . .

SMILLA
What were you supposed to do? Leave me there?

MORITZ
I punished you . . . because your mother was dead . . . I'd look at you and I'd see her face. I never loved anyone the way I loved your mother . . .

SMILLA
Benja will be sorry to hear that!

MORITZ
It's late, Smilla. I'm going to bed.
He gets up and leaves the room.

INT. MECHANIC'S CAR—LATE DUSK

He is wearing a suit, looks very handsome. Smilla is also dressed up. They are shy in this new incarnation. After a moment Smilla leans in to him, begins to kiss his neck.

SMILLA
All day today I've thought about your hands on me . . . Your mouth on my mouth . . .
He turns to kiss her, turns back to the road. She kisses him again.

DISSOLVE TO:
EXT. CASINO—NIGHT

The casino is on the sound, across from the water, in a private park. Many luxury cars are being parked, Rolls-Royces and Bentleys and Mercedeses. Smilla and the Mechanic exit his car and move toward the entrance.

SMILLA
This friend of yours . . . what does he do?

MECHANIC
Lander? He owns the place.

INT. CASINO—NIGHT

Smilla, the Mechanic, and BIRGO LANDER sit at the bar in the casino, crowded with dressed-up guests.

LANDER
Now, what can I do for you?

SMILLA
I need to know where the boat is going, why it's going, who's behind it.
He sighs, smiles at her.

LANDER
The ship you saw, the *Kronos*, is classified ice-class. They've spent an incredible amount of money getting her ready. I can tell you that whatever they're after, it has to be very lucrative for them to recoup the investment they've made.

SMILLA
But you don't know what it is?

LANDER
Normally a ship is chartered with a crew. But in this particular situation you would probably prefer a "bare boat" charter. Which means that you hire a ship and nothing else. Then you find a captain. He has to be a special kind of person, the kind you can take aside and, over a full glass, tell him that in this case his wages will be a little out of the ordinary. On the other hand, you need all his tact and sensitivity.

SMILLA
Where would someone find such a person?

LANDER
Right here.
From where they are sitting, Lander points out a man sitting at one of the blackjack tables: a perfect Slavic face, high cheekbones, black hair.
He's maybe in his early forties. He watches the dealer with absolute, focused attention.

LANDER
That German gentleman over there. Captain Sigmund Lukas. A very, very skillful seaman. Knows the North Atlantic like no one else. Doesn't drink. But he gambles. He no longer has a home or a 3family. And now he's reached the point where he's for sale. If the amount is big enough.

SMILLA
If he's so broke, whose money is he playing with?

LANDER
Uncle Lander's money, honey. That's why he's going to be nice to you . . .

INT. CASINO—NIGHT

Smilla is sitting next to Lukas at the table, her back to the room.

Across the room, as Birgo Lander surveys his domain, the Mechanic keeps a watchful eye on Smilla.

Lucas chain-smokes, drinks coffee. He never stops playing blackjack, and never once looks at Smilla as he talks.

LUKAS
One night in winter they come to me here. They ask me how I feel about the sea north of Nuuk in March. "Just like everybody else," I say, "I think

it's hell." I try to tell them about the pack ice and the icebergs. They pay no attention. They already know all about it. "How good are you?" they ask. "How good is your checkbook?" I say.

SMILLA
Who were they? Where are they going?

LUKAS
(*Shrugs.*)
I only know the ship. A coaster. Four thousand tons. The *Kronos*. Docked in South Harbor. We leave tonight.
As Smilla registers the fact it is leaving that night . . .

SMILLA
Can I come aboard?
The Mechanic practically lifts her out of her seat, walks her away from the table, to a far corner of the room. She is livid, tries to break free of him.

MECHANIC
This isn't a game. If you go on that boat, they'll kill you.

SMILLA
I need to know what happened to him.

MECHANIC
You don't even know where the boat is going.
Smilla regards him for a moment.

SMILLA
Wherever the boat is going, I'll find out why they killed Isaiah.
Suddenly the Mechanic pulls Smilla by the arm, propelling her forward. He has been watching two cops who have come into the casino a few minutes earlier. Now they make their move and secure the back door. Smilla is about to wrestle free again when he grabs her firmly.

MECHANIC
They've come for you. Just keep walking—don't turn around.
Smilla starts to walk through the casino, the Mechanic directly behind her. Straight ahead is the door to the foyer. From either side, Ravn and two other policemen close in fast. Smilla forces her feet to move. They finally make it through the foyer door. The Mechanic stops, picks up a pole, and uses it to secure the doors—creating a solid bar by running it through the handles.

    A heavy thud as the men start to bang against the door.

MECHANIC
Lander will be waiting outside . . .
Smilla turns to face him.

MECHANIC
Go to your father's house and wait there. I'll meet you there—
As the men start to break the door, the Mechanic

braces himself against it, holds it shut a moment longer.

MECHANIC
Go—go—
She kisses him quickly and then turns away and is out the door, running down the gravel path.

EXT. CASINO. LANDER'S BMW—NIGHT

Smilla gets into Lander's car. They drive off.

INT. LANDER'S BMW—NIGHT

SMILLA
I need you to help me get on the *Kronos*.
Lander looks at her for a moment.

LANDER
What makes you think I can help?

SMILLA
Just talk to Lukas . . .
He laughs. Smilla stares straight ahead.

LANDER
My life is shit. But whatever it's worth I owe to your boyfriend. So the answer is no.
Smilla is quiet for a long moment.

SMILLA
I'm going whether you help me or not.

INT. LANDER'S BMW—NIGHT

Smilla and Lander pull up on a dark suburban street. Smilla is about to get out of the car when Lander stops her.

LANDER
Wait . . . wait . . .
He hands her a card with a phone number and then sighs deeply.

LANDER
You scare me, honey. Other women, it's all threat and no action. You I believe. You'll go anyway and get yourself really fucked. So, give me a call when you're ready.
She turns to him with gratitude, kisses him.

SMILLA
Thank you, Lander.

EXT. MORITZ'S HOUSE—NIGHT

Smilla is about to enter the backyard leading to Moritz's house when something makes her stop. We see, between the two pillars flanking the front drive, a sort of fog. Nothing else. But it is enough for Smilla to flatten herself against the wall of the house and wait. After a moment, she sees the detective from the rooftop talking to another POLICE-MAN. She skirts the house and runs down the basement stairs.

INT. MORITZ'S HOUSE. HALL/KITCHEN—NIGHT

Smilla waits just outside the kitchen, where Benja is talking to Ravn. She is seeing him out.

BENJA
Thank you very much . . . It's the door straight ahead.
Smilla comes into the kitchen, comes up close to Benja.

SMILLA
Benja . . .

*Benja twirls around, startled out of her wits to see
Smilla. She is about to scream when Smilla clamps a
hand around her mouth. As she propels her into the
living room . . .*

INT. MORITZ'S HOUSE. LIVING ROOM/HALL—NIGHT

*Moritz looks up from his reading. Smilla lets go of
Benja, who goes and stands next to him.*

BENJA
You don't belong here. They're going to take you
away.
*Smilla looks at her father. He can barely look at her
his guilt is so extreme.*

MORITZ
You can't run from everything your whole life.
We'll get you a good lawyer. The best. We'll have
you out . . .
Smilla comes close to him.

SMILLA
Listen to me. They'll find a way to kill me—I'll just
have an accident . . . I was resisting arrest, I tried to
escape. And you'll spend the rest of your wretched
life knowing you could have saved me.
Benja can see him weakening.

BENJA
Are you going out to them yourself, or should I get
them?

MORITZ
Just give us a minute, please.

BENJA
You promised me. She's crazy! I can't take this
anymore.
He stands up suddenly and turns to Benja.

MORITZ
(Yells at her.)
Will you be quiet!
*Benja is so unaccustomed to this she is momentarily
rendered mute. Moritz and Smilla move to the hall-
way.*

MORITZ
What do you want me to do?

SMILLA
Drive your car up to the back door. As close as possible, so I can get in and lie on the floor. And then
cover me.
*He moves off to do this. Smilla picks up the phone
in the hallway and dials the number Lander gave
her.*

LANDER'S VOICE
Lander here.

SMILLA
Where are you?

LANDER'S VOICE
Meet me at the boat.

SMILLA
Thank you, Lander. I'm coming.
Then she hangs up. When she turns around, Benja is behind her.

BENJA
Once you drive off, I'll send them after you.
Smilla steps close to her, grabs Benja by the crotch, through her leotard, and squeezes. She pushes her against the table, holds her there. When she opens her mouth to scream, Smilla puts her other hand around her throat and cuts off her windpipe.

SMILLA
(Whispers.)
Benja—leave me alone.
Smilla holds on to her, her eyes bulging, until she is totally subdued. Then Smilla lowers her to the floor, where she sits staring blankly.

EXT. MORITZ'S HOUSE—NIGHT

Moritz backs his car out of the garage. Ravn comes up to the car. Moritz pushes a button and the window glides down.

MORITZ
An emergency at the hospital . . .
Ravn steps closer to the car. For a moment it looks as if he will check it, then he backs away.

MORITZ
Good night. Thanks for your help.
And then they drive through the gate.

INT. MORITZ'S CAR—NIGHT

Smilla is sitting next to her father as he drives toward the city.

MORITZ
I wanted peace and quiet so badly. I wanted to have my family around me. But I never achieved that. I don't want to let you go, Smilla.
Smilla sits quietly, then reaches over and takes his hand. They drive in silence.

EXT. WATER SKI CLUB—NIGHT

Lander is busy getting a small yacht ready to go. Moritz waits by his car, approaches her . . .
    Smilla hugs him goodbye.
    Moritz holds on to her, and finally Landers comes and pulls Smilla away, settles her in the boat, and then starts it, fast. Smilla turns and watches as her father goes back to his car. And she continues to watch until she can't see him anymore.

INT. LANDER'S BOAT—NIGHT

Landers maneuvers the boat through the rough swells with great authority.
    Suddenly the enormous ship, the Kronos, *materializes out of the fog. The tanker is huge and ominous-looking . . .*

LANDER
Change your mind and come back with me.

SMILLA
No, thank you.
She turns and regards the vast floating hulk of the Kronos.

EXT. *KRONOS*—NIGHT

Smilla climbs up a small ladder to the ship as Lander's yacht can be seen heading back to the harbor.

The promising young German actor Jürgen Vogel plays Jakkelsen

INT. *KRONOS*. KITCHEN—DAWN

The kitchen is full of people when Smilla enters.

JAKKELSEN
I've been waiting for you.
JAKKELSEN—a redheaded, freckled, skinny boy who sits smoking a cigarette with his feet up on a table.

149

JAKKELSEN
Nils Jakkelsen.
He looks her over.

JAKKELSEN
Stick with me, because I can do things for you, you
know what I mean?

SMILLA
You can start by getting my bag.
*She drops it on the table, causing his feet to fly up in
the air and his chair to go over. He gets up off the
floor, wary—and takes her bag. She follows him out
of the room.*

JAKKELSEN
The captain wants to see you . . .

EXT. *KRONOS*. DECK—DAWN

*Jakkelsen leads the way along the main deck, Smilla
taking in the ship's geography. White floodlights
line the rails . . . massive cargo booms are poised
above the sealed cargo holds—the ship has an
almost military feel to it.*

JAKKELSEN
To your left . . . upstairs . . .
*They climb a level to the navigation deck, passing a
cordoned-off flight of steps with the notice
STRICTLY NO ADMITTANCE.*

INT. *KRONOS*. WHEELHOUSE—DAWN

JAKKELSEN
It's in there.
*Smilla enters the wheelhouse. The standard radar
and sonar equipment is augmented with high-tech
navigational aids and other mysterious consoles of
lights. Standing at the wheel is Captain Lukas. He
barely glances at Jakkelsen.*

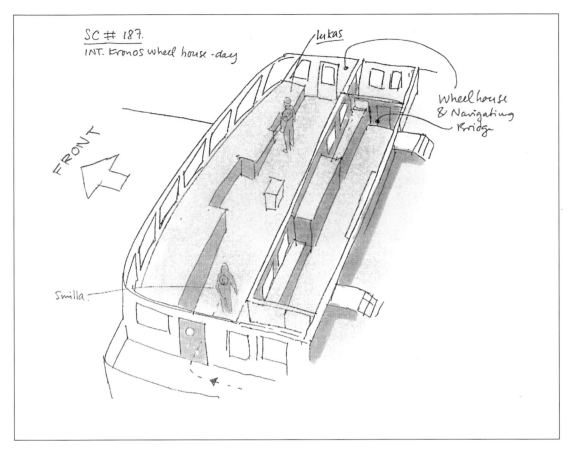

Simon Bang's drawing shows the geography of the Kronos's *bridge*

LUKAS
You can go, Jakkelsen.
Jakkelsen disappears.

LUKAS
(Without looking at Smilla)
You're on board because we needed a cabin
steward. Your duties include light cleaning, and
you're responsible for the ship's laundry. The conversation we had in the casino was an employment
interview, nothing else. You can go now.
As she turns to leave . . .

LUKAS
We have representatives from the shipping company with us. They live on the upper boat deck.

There's no admittance whatsoever. If you disobey this order, I'll have you locked up.
Smilla is about to reply, thinks better of it. She goes, leaving Lukas with his gaze fixed on the horizon.

EXT. *KRONOS*. DECK—DAWN

Smilla climbs down from the bridge and starts to walk back along the deck, memorizing every inch. Jakkelsen's been waiting for her. As she enters the cabin passage . . .

INT. *KRONOS*. CABIN CORRIDOR—DAWN

. . . Jakkelsen catches up to her, opens her door with a master key from a large bunch of keys jangling from his belt.

JAKKELSEN
My cabin is next door if you need anything.

EXT. *KRONOS* AND OCEAN—DAWN

Shot from high above as it makes its way out of the channel now and out into the vast open sea.

INT. *KRONOS*. SMILLA'S CABIN—DAWN

Jakkelsen opens the door to Smilla's small cabin, carries her bag inside, then steps out again to let her enter. There's a washroom and a shower, a small metal bunk, a locker, a desk, and a porthole. Smilla, exhausted, watches as he puts the huge ring of keys back on his belt.

JAKKELSEN
How about a quick fuck?
In reply, Smilla sticks out her foot and slams the door. It just misses Jakkelsen's face as he jumps back.

JAKKELSEN
(Through the door)
Women are crazy about me.
Jakkelsen whistles as he walks off.

EXT. *KRONOS*. BOAT DECK—DAY

*Smilla moves along the boat deck, carrying a mop
and pail and dressed in a uniform of blue pants and
a jacket. She leans back against the rail, trying to
see the upper deck—and how to reach it. Compan-
ionways, but they're all cordoned off. Then she
notices a door marked FORWARD CARGO
HOLD. Making sure no one is watching, she tries
the door. It's firmly locked.*

EXT. *KRONOS*. COVERED DECK—DAY

*Smilla walks along the covered B deck, sees a door
marked ENGINE ROOM.*

INT. *KRONOS*. ENGINE ROOM—DAY

*Deafening noise: pistons pumping, valves vibrating,
steam pouring out.
    Smilla walks along a steel walkway—one of
several at each deck level. Far below, the engine
roars. Everywhere, signs prohibit smoking in five
languages. Up ahead, Smilla sees an alcove. As she
moves into it she sees Jakkelsen, his feet up on a
worktable, splicing cable. When he sees it's Smilla
he reaches up to one of the smoke detectors directly
above him and covers it with a napkin, then lights
the cigar hanging out of his mouth.*

JAKKELSEN
(Smiling)
Smilla *Qaavigaaq* Jaspersen. That must be a Green-
landic middle name.

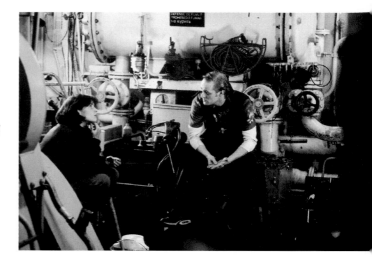

*Smilla ignores him and sits down. He wants to
talk, seems to be in a state of barely controlled
nervous excitement.*

SMILLA
What's in the forward cargo hold?

JAKKELSEN
Fuck if I know, man. I've been sailing for five years,
I know everything about ships, and I've never seen
security like this before.

SMILLA
You've got all the keys. Why not take a look?

JAKKELSEN
Not to the cargo hold. This whole outfit is weird.
Even the captain says he doesn't know where we're
headed. Then there's the crew. They're a pile of shit.
And they stick together. And they're scared. I can't
get them to tell me why. And then the passengers
upstairs we never get to see. Who the fuck are they?

153

He puts down his cigar. Smilla says nothing. She spots a tin full of large ball bearings and secretes one without Jakkelsen seeing.

JAKKELSEN
Then there's you, Smilla . . . Why'd Lukas let you on board? Everyone thinks you're a cop. Is that what you're doing here, spying on me?
Smilla stands up to leave.

SMILLA
Actually, Jakkelsen, I came for a quick fuck. But you spoiled it by talking.
Then, without warning, Smilla grabs one of his skinny arms. She pushes up the sleeve, sees the yellow and blue needle marks all along the inside of his elbow. Then she drops his arm and leaves.

INT. *KRONOS*. MESSROOM—EVENING

A cartoon is playing on a TV set in the messroom.
Most of the crew is there, including Jakkelsen, who laughs louder than anyone, his appreciation of

Tom and Jerry having received a recent shot in the arm. Smilla sits behind him, eyeing his jacket on the floor. Jerry fires a rocket down Tom's throat. Smilla steals Jakkelsen's bunch of keys as he howls with glee.

INT. *KRONOS*. JAKKELSEN'S CABIN—EVENING

Tight: Hands search little drawers: letters, razor blades, foreign coins, a dog-eared and much thumbed porno magazine. Several of them. Identity papers. A box of chess pieces, gold chains like the ones he wears, cologne. Next, his shelf. Dictionaries, a couple of books on chess. A paperback entitled Flossy—Sweet Sixteen.
Smilla goes to Jakkelsen's bunk and lies down. Closes her eyes and tries to find the junkie in herself. Opens her eyes and sees a knife sticking out of his drawer. On the edge of the blade are a few tiny bottle-green specks.
Smilla gets up and rifles through his locker. No clothes in that color. Goes back to the desk by his bed. Takes a chess piece from the box, turns it over: the base is lined with green felt.
The blade eases between the felt and the base of the black bishop, exposing a small metal disk. Smilla eases it free, and out falls a plastic tube. She's already collected several others: rooks, knights, kings, and queens.

INT. *KRONOS*. MESSROOM—EVENING

The movie has ended. A hyper Jakkelsen leaves the messroom.

INT. *KRONOS*. CABIN CORRIDOR—EVENING

Smilla leaves Jakkelsen's cabin and enters her own.

INT. *KRONOS*. SMILLA'S CABIN— EVENING

Smilla takes the stolen steel ball bearing and wraps it in a white towel, twisting it so that the ball rests securely inside the towel, the ends hanging free.

INT. *KRONOS*. CABIN CORRIDOR— EVENING

Jakkelsen grabs for the key to his cabin on his belt—discovers it is gone. Is surprised and puzzled to see it in his door.

INT. *KRONOS*. SMILLA'S CABIN— EVENING

Smilla hangs the towel over the sink, arranging it so it falls naturally. Then she sits down on the bunk to wait, knowing he will come. There is nothing more predictable than a junkie.

INT. *KRONOS*. JAKKELSEN'S CABIN— EVENING

He enters his room. Senses someone has been there, sits down, and removes the felt from the chess pieces —discovers that the dope is gone.

INT. *KRONOS*. SMILLA'S CABIN— EVENING

Smilla waits on her bunk, listens to him as he starts to tear his cabin apart, searching for his dope.

INT. *KRONOS*. JAKKELSEN'S CABIN— EVENING

Jakkelsen stops, sits down on his bunk. Stands up again. He takes a steel spike from his drawer and tiptoes out of his room.

INT. *KRONOS*. CABIN CORRIDOR— EVENING

Jakkelsen stands outside Smilla's door.

INT. *KRONOS*. SMILLA'S CABIN— EVENING

Smilla stands by the door, can hear him outside her cabin. Both of them wait, trying to control their breath. Smilla leans forward to turn out the light and this is the moment he's been waiting for. He opens it so that it strikes her on the temple and knocks her to the floor between the bunk and the locker. He comes inside, shuts the door. He's carrying the huge steel spike.

JAKKELSEN
Give it here.
Smilla tries to sit up.

JAKKELSEN
Stay down!
He slams her in the foot with the spike. She gasps with the astonishing pain as it hits the bone.

JAKKELSEN
Give it to me.
Smilla puts her hand in her pocket and pulls out one of the tubes. He grabs it from her.

JAKKELSEN
All of it.

SMILLA
In the cabin.

JAKKELSEN
No, no. You get it out for me.
Smilla pulls herself up, using the sink. She takes the white towel from the sink and wipes the blood off

205	218	INT	CABIN AND BATHROOM Hides in shower, gets wet, Mechanic disarms her, make love	Night	1 3/8 pgs.	1, 2
206	220	INT	CABIN AND BATHROOM Talk about the expedition.	Dawn	1 3/8 pgs.	1, 2
269	New Scene	INT	CABIN AND BATHROOM Mechanic checks Diving kit.	Night	1/8 pgs.	2
207	222	INT	CORRIDOR AND STAIRS Maurice, Smilla fight, Mechanic Ko's him, hides body, they go	Dawn	6/8 pgs.	1, 2, 20
--- END OF DAY 54 -- Wed, May 22, 1996 -- 3 6/8 pgs.						
194	194	INT	UPPER DECK SALON Steals across room, close to killing Tork goes on hearing nois	Night	3/8 pgs.	1, 4
191	190,196	INT	UPPER DECK KITCHENETTE LAB From dumbwaiter crosses room, Runs to dumbwaiter	Night	2/8 pgs.	1
249	191	INT	UPPER DECK LABORATORY Searches room takes map and cassette, puts on video.	Night	3/8 pgs.	1
250	193	INT	UPPER DECK LABORATORY Horrified, removes tape leaves room.	Night	3/8 pgs.	1
268	New Scene	INT	KRONOS T.B.A. Tork at work	Night	1/8 pgs.	4
--- END OF DAY 55 -- Thu, May 23, 1996 -- 1 4/8 pgs.						
164	159	INT	KRONOS CABBINS PASSAGE Shows her to her cabin.	Dawn	1/8 pgs.	1, 7
168	160	INT	KRONOS SMILLAS CABIN Is shown her cabin.	Dawn	3/8 pgs.	1, 7
169	168,170	INT	KRONOS SMILLAS CABIN Wraps ballbearings in towel, hangs towel by sink.	Night	2/8 pgs.	1
169A	172,175	INT	KRONOS SMILLAS CABIN Listens to J next door, Smilla by door listening.	Night	1/8 pgs.	1
170	177	INT	KRONOS SMILLAS CABIN Jakkelsen bursts in, they fight.	Night	7/8 pgs.	1, 7
171	178	INT	KRONOS SMILLAS CABIN Smilla wants keys to kargo hold.	Night	4/8 pgs.	1, 7
172	211	INT	KRONOS SMILLAS CABIN Packing to leave ship.	Night	1/8 pgs.	1, 7
--- END OF DAY 56 -- Fri, May 24, 1996 -- 3 1/8 pgs.						
95	195	INT	UPPER DECK LAB/ SALON Peers through crack in door.	Night	1/8 pgs.	1, 5
248	198,199	INT	UPPER DECK KITCHENETTE See's Lquen Enter, He's distracted by tv.	Night	4/8 pgs.	1, 5
189	183	INT	REFRIGERATION HOLD They see the net.	Night	3/8 pgs.	1, 7
187	182	INT	FORWARD CARGO HOLD In awe of what they see.	Night	1/8 pgs.	1, 7
188	203	INT	FORWARD CARGO HOLD Jakkelsen shows the heroin.	Night	4/8 pgs.	1, 7
--- END OF DAY 57 -- Sat, May 25, 1996 -- 2 3/8 pgs.						
Sun, May 26, 1996, REST DAY						
Mon, 27, May, 1996, PUBLIC HOLIDAY (Whitsun)						
181	169	INT	KRONOS MESS ROOM Show ends Jakkelsen leaves.	Night	1/8 pgs.	7, 19, 20
179	165	INT	KRONOS MESS ROOM Steals Jakkelsens keys.	Night	2/8 pgs.	1, 7, 19, 20
180	167	INT	KRONOS MESS ROOM Returns Jakkelsens keys.	Night	1/8 pgs.	1, 7, 19, 20

(LEFT AND ABOVE) *The shooting schedule is set up by the first assistant director in close collaboration with the production department and the director. Many things must be considered, for example: When can we shoot where? Is it day or night, winter or summer? Which actors are available on which days? A complicated jigsaw puzzle*

her face. Then, *still carrying the towel, she turns back, starting her swing. He expects the towel, not the heavy steel ball wrapped in it that sends him to his knees. He touches his mouth, spits blood into his hand, along with a few pieces of something lighter-colored.*

JAKKELSEN
(Lisping through broken tooth)
You've ruined my face.
Half of a front tooth is missing.

JAKKELSEN
Give me the dope, Smilla.

SMILLA
Not until we've seen the forward cargo hold. Or I'll tell Lukas what a little needle freak you are.

JAKKELSEN
I told you. I don't have the key.

SMILLA
You'll think of something, Jakkelsen.

EXT. *KRONOS*—NIGHT

The Kronos *is sailing through the ice in the dark of the night.*

INT. *KRONOS*. WHEELHOUSE AND CORRIDOR—NIGHT

We can just make out Lukas in the distance, standing at the wheel with his back to us. Jakkelsen watches him briefly, then very quietly opens the hatch to a small cupboard and takes out a set of keys.

EXT. *KRONOS*. FORWARD DECK— NIGHT

The weather has got worse: driving rain and a pitching sea. A shaking Jakkelsen tries various combinations of keys on the door to the forward hold. Success as the door swings open.

INT. *KRONOS*. FORWARD CARGO HOLD— NIGHT

They are at the top of a metal stairway. Jakkelsen closes the door behind them while Smilla shines a powerful flashlight over the hold below.

Jakkelsen lets out a low whistle of astonishment. The hold is filled with huge, reinforced-steel holding tanks; stacks of narrow-gauge rails—straight and curved; piles of thick wooden railroad ties chained into huge bundles . . . and a helicopter.

They climb down the metal gantry and into the hold. Smilla opens the door to one of the steel storage tanks, shines her flashlight over diving equipment: tanks, helmets, respirators, netting bags, air balloons, weights, suits with specially protected seams . . .

JAKKELSEN
What the fuck is all this shit? This is giving me the creeps, man.
Smilla looks around. She opens a tank. It is filled with equipment more at home in a particle accelerator chamber than a tanker: radiation detectors,

PET and QUEST electron scanners, portable sonar imaging devices . . . and a huge spherical gyroscope made of metal arcs fitted with electron emitters and receivers.

Smilla moves to a heavy metal door flanked with

the deck. A crew member, HANSEN, stands in the foreground, watching them, cleaning his nails with a knife.

INT. *KRONOS*. CABIN CORRIDOR—NIGHT

Smilla unlocks her cabin, Jakkelsen whispering from behind.

JAKKELSEN
I'm telling you, man—this whole thing is costing them millions . . . Dope's the only thing that can finance this shit.

SMILLA
You have dope on the brain, sweet sixteen.
He holds out his hand for one of his tubes. Smilla gives it to him and closes the door on him, Jakkelsen calling out:

JAKKELSEN
When I jerk off tonight, Smilla, I'll be thinking of you.

EXT. *KRONOS* AND OCEAN—DAY

From out of thick mist looms the spectral Kronos, sailing through a still and shrouded sea.
    As Smilla glides by, we hear the icy wind howling through the rigging. She moves along the deck, a tiny figure huddled against the freezing wind, carrying a tray up to the bridge. She glances at the upper deck above her, but there seems to be no way of getting up there.

INT. *KRONOS*. KITCHEN—NIGHT

Jakkelsen looks inside the dumbwaiter, stacked with a tray of dirty dishes—then looks at us.

thermostat controls. She looks through a window in the door.

INT. *KRONOS*. REFRIGERATION HOLD—NIGHT

Smilla gazes down at a vast refrigeration hold. It is empty except for a huge net, hanging from the roof and swinging from side to side with the movement of the ship. Jakkelsen moves up beside her.

JAKKELSEN
It's a dope run, man. I know everything about the sea. That's why we're all getting paid triple rate—to keep our mouths shut.

SMILLA
Looks to me like they want to bring something back. Something big. Maybe something alive.

EXT. *KRONOS*. MAIN DECK—NIGHT

Smilla and Jakkelsen make their way back along

JAKKELSEN
No way! I get claustrophobic. I'm not kidding.
Smilla is standing behind him. She unloads the tray.

SMILLA
That's why I'm going.

JAKKELSEN
I get claustrophobic for other people, too, man!
*Smilla opens a drawer and finds a screwdriver. She
takes a cork from a bottle and corks the screwdriver, then tucks it into the waistband of her pants,
before folding herself into the dumbwaiter, her
knees up against her chest.*

SMILLA
Press the button for the upper deck. If anyone tries
to send you away, refuse to leave. Give me an hour.
If I'm not back in an hour, wake up Lukas.

JAKKELSEN
(Panicked)
I can't do that, man.

SMILLA
Why not?

JAKKELSEN
He's my father. That's why I'm on board . . . That's
why I have the key. He thinks I'm clean . . .
Smilla studies him for a moment.

JAKKELSEN
(Shocked)
You'd do that to me, man? You'd tell him?

SMILLA
In a second.

JAKKELSEN
After everything I've done for you?

SMILLA
Now send me up.
*Smilla scrunches herself up, her knees to her chest
with her head between them. Jakkelsen closes the
door and hits the button.*

INT. *KRONOS*. DUMBWAITER—NIGHT

*The motor rumbles to life and the dumbwaiter
begins its jerky ascent. Cables strain with the extra
weight, drawing it up toward us. Beyond it: a ver-
tiginous drop to the bottom. Smilla's starting to get
claustrophobic: there's no room for movement
inside this tiny box, and it rattles from side to side
with every sway of the boat.*

    Finally it staggers to a halt.

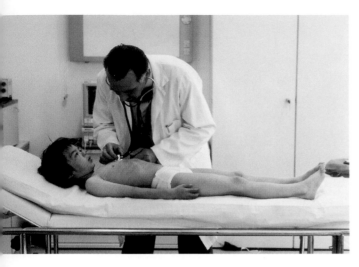

INT. *KRONOS*. UPPER DECK. KITCHENETTE /LABORATORY—NIGHT

The tip of the screwdriver wiggles between the little doors, frantically trying to force them open. Finally Smilla appears, heaving a sigh of relief. She slips out into a modern, well-equipped kitchenette, then heads for the corridor.

INT. *KRONOS*. UPPER DECK. LABORATORY —NIGHT

Smilla enters a large laboratory, partitioned off from a room beyond it that lies hidden behind mahogany doors. The lab is filled with equipment: microscopes, core samples, steel maps. Smilla studies them. One of them shows the exact location of the Gela Alta glacier. She takes it from its holder, folds it, and pockets it. Her eye falls on an aquarium. She reads a note on it: NO SALT WATER! She also sees a small stack of videotapes; labels tell us they are from the Institute for Arctic Medicine. And

something else now: the cassette tape that belonged to Isaiah. Smilla now knows without a shadow of a doubt that the men have killed him for it. She pockets it as well. Takes one of the videotapes and puts it into the monitor. Watches the following image:

INT. INSTITUTE FOR ARCTIC MEDICINE— DAY

Isaiah, terrified, is lying on a examination table as a blood sample is being taken from his arm by Loyen.

CUT TO:
Tørk sitting at a desk, interrogating Isaiah.

TØRK
Where is the tape?
(And again, this time louder)
Where is the tape?

INT. *KRONOS*. LABORATORY—NIGHT

Smilla horrified, reaches up and removes the tape. Stands for a long moment thinking about Isaiah and what they've done to him. She moves toward the mahogany doors. Pushes them open.

INT. *KRONOS*. UPPER DECK. SALON— NIGHT

The walls are all paneled in the same dark, beautiful wood. Leather club chairs are placed next to reading lamps. Books line the shelves. Smilla moves toward one of the chairs, approaches the back of it. A man is in one of them, his feet out in front of him, resting on a matching ottoman. Smilla moves toward him quietly, comes around to face him now. Tørk is sleeping peacefully, his white hair loose; he looks handsome in this light. Smilla steps closer to him, watches him for a long moment. Time is

suspended. She leans in closer, almost as if she is going to kiss him. She listens to his breathing, sees the steady pulse in his neck. It is only as she is inches from him that we see the screwdriver in her hand, poised an inch away from the pulse, where the blood pounds through his body. She raises the screwdriver, is arrested at the last moment by the sound of someone outside the door. Smilla lowers the screwdriver and quickly goes into the laboratory.

INT. *KRONOS*. LABORATORY/SALOON— NIGHT

Smilla peers through the partly closed door into the saloon and sees Loyen enter carrying an empty champagne bottle. She turns.

INT. *KRONOS*. UPPER DECK. KITCHENETTE —NIGHT

Smilla runs back to the kitchenette. She rings the bell of the dumbwaiter.

INT. *KRONOS*. KITCHEN—NIGHT

The shrill sound of the bell ringing out into the empty room. Jakkelsen is gone.

INT. *KRONOS*. UPPER DECK. KITCHENETTE —NIGHT

Smilla slips inside the dumbwaiter and tries to close the doors from the inside, but it's impossible to close them completely.

    Through the crack of the dumbwaiter doors Smilla sees Loyen enter the kitchenette carrying the empty champagne bottle. He goes straight toward the dumbwaiter. *Smilla curls even smaller, screwdriver at the ready. Loyen has almost reached the dumbwaiter when he is distracted by the atmospheric sound of the TV monitor Smilla had left on. He looks at the atmospheric picture on the monitor and the open cover on the table. With one hand he thrusts the bottle into the dumbwaiter.*

    Smilla holds her breath in terror as he puts the bottle in her lap.

    But he doesn't see her, just pushes the down button, the doors close, and the dumbwaiter jerks into action.

INT. *KRONOS*. KITCHEN—NIGHT

*The doors open and Smilla senses someone there,
stabs out with the screwdriver, almost impaling the
cook, URS: half-asleep, astonished. She misses him
by inches. He has come to check on his baking
bread. He looks at Smilla, in surprise. She hands
him the bottle.*

SMILLA
They're out of champagne.

EXT. *KRONOS*—DAY

From high above, we see the Kronos *plow through
huge, rough swells.*

EXT. *KRONOS*. BOAT DECK—DAY

*The weather is horrible: heavy torrential rain,
whipped around by the wind. Huge ice floes now,
as long as the ship. Smilla comes out of a door onto
the deck, and when she realizes how deserted it is,
she turns to go back. The door bangs behind her as
Hansen follows her through. She turns around,
starts to run, and then sees MAURICE moving
toward her. She is trapped between them now.*

*Maurice stops as Hansen comes closer. Smilla
goes over to the rail and looks down at the sea forty
feet below. And then she sees two ropes attached to
the outside of the ship. She gets up on the rail and
Hansen rushes for her. He tries to grab her, but at
that moment the* Kronos *is struck by a heavy swell
and the hull shudders and lists, making him let go.
Smilla starts to climb down.*

*Smilla reaches the windows of the promenade
deck. She sees Verlaine behind the window; he sees
Smilla but just, very calmly, closes the curtains.
Smilla reaches the deck below. Limping, she runs
toward the engine room door.*

SC #209 INT. KRONOS. Engine Room Day.

Wide shot Engine Room
Smilla running on the
top steel platform.
Hansen below her, running
after her.

INT. *KRONOS*. CORRIDOR LEADING TO ENGINE ROOM—DAY

*Smilla runs through the corridor, hears the door
behind her clang open. Hansen is catching up with
her. She opens a door to escape, but behind it is
Maurice. Then, suddenly, everything goes black.*

*Smilla: inside the blanket they've thrown over
her, desperately trying to free one of her hands . . .*

They carry her into the engine room along the steel platform that goes around the room. Far below, the roar of the engine. They take her to the highest point, where there is the longest drop down to the engine. Smilla is desperately struggling to get free.

HANSEN
I'll go down and make sure she's dead when she hits the bottom.
Hansen leaves. Maurice is having problems holding Smilla and gives her a blow on the head. For a moment she doesn't move.

And just as Maurice is about to drop her, Smilla stabs through the blanket with her screwdriver, right into the soft space between his neck and shoulder.

Maurice drops her and staggers back, the wound oozing blood between his fingers.

Smilla: inside the blanket. And then the sound starts, a relentless high-pitched scream.

Smilla thinks it's Maurice screaming. Then someone grabs her by the shoulders and starts to drag her. She is released. The relentless screaming and another sound now . . . An animal next to her is coughing up its lungs. Smilla works the blanket off herself and realizes the animal next to her is Jakkelsen, panting for air. Overhead, the sprinkler system is sending gallons of water down on them.

JAKKELSEN
What else could I do? I lit a cigar and put my mouth at the sensor. Then the shit hit the fan. I'm really fucked now—they know it's me, man.
He runs off, and a moment later Urs and the engineer, KÜTZOW, appear, dressed in full firefighting gear with oxygen tanks. Smilla stands up, almost falls over, then staggers off. They move to let her past.

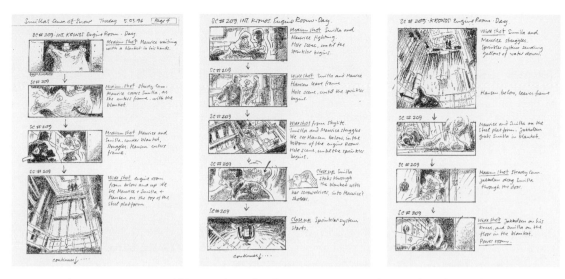

(ABOVE) *Fighting scenes are incredibly complicated and time-consuming to shoot and an almost choreographic preparation is necessary with the help of a stunt coordinator. Again, storyboards are very useful, as the drawings clearly show what the director has in mind*

INT. *KRONOS*. CABIN CORRIDOR—NIGHT

Smilla and Jakkelsen are running back through the cabin passage.

JAKKELSEN
Bunch of freaks. What the hell did you do to them, they want to kill you?

SMILLA
(Yells.)
They want to kill both of us . . .

EXT. *KRONOS*—NIGHT

The Kronos *is approaching the Nordic Star: a floating industrial monster of an oil rig that rises out of the ocean . . . a belching vision of hell.*

INT. *KRONOS*. SMILLA'S CABIN—NIGHT

A badly frightened Smilla is packing her duffel bag as Jakkelsen watches her. He sees the desperation in her eyes. Suddenly there is an announcement that booms out over the P.A. system in the cabin:

LUKAS'S VOICE
This is the captain. We're approaching the Nordic Star platform. We'll be docked for about half an hour. All crew members are confined to quarters. No one is to leave the ship. I repeat: No one is to leave the ship.

SMILLA
We've got to get off the ship now.

JAKKELSEN
Don't look so panicky, man. Just stick close to Jakkelsen the Great. Ever been to Hong Kong?

LUKAS'S VOICE
This is a supply stopover.

JAKKELSEN
They offered me a modeling contract once. Let's go there.

LUKAS'S VOICE
You are expressly refused permission to leave the ship. Any crew member attempting to do so will be arrested and taken into custody.

SMILLA
Won't he worry about you?

JAKKELSEN
I'll send him a telegram. Let's get out of here.

DISSOLVE TO:
EXT. *KRONOS*/NORDIC STAR—NIGHT

They have now docked at the Nordic Star. It's like a huge city looming up out of the ocean—for drilling oil; built on pontoons in the middle of the ocean. Its piers are half a mile long, with signs that read: ACCESS TO PIER STRICTLY FORBIDDEN.

EXT. *KRONOS*. DECK—NIGHT

Smilla and Jakkelsen are hidden behind a tarp on deck.
    Hansen is sitting on the deck, just where the gangway starts, to ensure that no one leaves the ship. Past the gangway, a long pier, with lights along the length of it.

JAKKELSEN
How about a quick fuck before we go?
Smilla smiles. Then they watch Hansen. He is bored, tips his chair back, playing a game to see how far he can tip it back without going over. Jakkelsen pulls out a pair of wire cutters.

JAKKELSEN
Once the lights go out, give me a head start and then follow me.
Smilla reaches up a hand and touches his face in gratitude.

JAKKELSEN
Relax, man. You can make it up to me in Hong Kong.
He bites through the thick cable behind them with the wire cutters, and the lights go out. They can make out Hansen going over in his chair. Then he leaps to his feet and disappears in the darkness. Jakkelsen takes off.

EXT. *KRONOS*. DECK/PIER TO NORDIC STAR—NIGHT

Smilla waits, counting the seconds until he reappears again, madly sprinting along the long pier linking the ship and the Nordic Star. Every fifty feet along the pier, overhead lights illuminate a circle on the ground. Smilla sees Jakkelsen weave in and out of the lighted areas, and she is off, running down the gangway after him. She reaches the pier, and stops suddenly. Jakkelsen has disappeared. She stops, her heart pounding, and then is vastly relieved when she sees him again. She comes on, slows when he does. He is weaving now, lurching forward.

EXT. NORDIC STAR. PIER—NIGHT

Smilla runs after him, and finds him collapsed against a lamppost. He looks up at her, a goofy smile on his face.

SMILLA
Get up. We're almost there.

JAKKELSEN
I don't feel well.
Smilla tries to lift him, gets him to his feet, they stagger a few yards, and he sinks to his knees.

JAKKELSEN
Why'd you have to break my tooth? It'll be hard to find modeling jobs.
Smilla can't hold him, lets him go. She sees the blood pouring from his chest and pulls his jacket away from him. His heavy set of passkeys falls to the ground. When Smilla tries to stop the flow of blood with her fingers, they close around the knife sticking out of him.

JAKKELSEN
Never look right at the audience, man. You gotta look over their heads, proud, like you don't give a shit. Like a fucking star, man. Like a star.

SMILLA
Yes, Jakkelsen. Like a star.

He shudders convulsively as Smilla holds him. A moment later, he dies. Horrified, Smilla lets go of him and forces herself forward, toward the sanctuary of the Nordic Star and the cluster of buildings up ahead. She is almost at the end of the pier when huge floodlights come on. Smilla is blinded, moves forward a few feet. Stops, can just make out the silhouette of a figure moving toward her. It is so bright Smilla cannot see who it is. There is no way around the figure. Smilla is forced to turn around and run back to the boat. The figure comes on, seconds behind her.

INT. *KRONOS.* **DECK—NIGHT**

Using Jakkelsen's passkey, Smilla gains entry to the upper deck. She enters a dark corridor, presses herself against the wall when she sees a person farther down the corridor. She opens the door closest to her and enters a cabin.

INT. *KRONOS.* **CABIN—NIGHT**

When she hears someone coming and then the key opening the door, Smilla enters the bathroom and waits inside the shower stall, holding the screwdriver, her hands shaking.

A hand reaches in and turns on the faucets, adjusting the temperature. The water soaks her. Smilla still cannot see who it is.

A hand reaches in. Smilla waits, almost cries out now as the figure brushes his hand against her. Returns to her, feels her arm, takes the screwdriver from her. Turns on the light and draws the curtain away.

The Mechanic looks at the wet, bloody Smilla still standing in the shower. She is limp with fear, battle-weary. He puts a towel around his waist.

SMILLA
What are they paying you? Is it enough?
A long moment before he answers her.

MECHANIC
The g-g-government never pays very much.
Smilla goes to slam him across the face; he catches her hand, pins it back. She flails at him; he takes her arms, holds them so she can't strike out again.

MECHANIC
Listen to me—the government knew something big was going on. They didn't know what it was ex-

actly, but they knew they were going again. They hired me because I was a diver. Because I was the kind of person that Tørk needed. I met him. He trusted me. He arranged for me to move into the building so that I could keep an eye on the boy.
(Beat)
I didn't know he was sick.
She goes to hit him again, starts to cry.

SMILLA
You never loved him?

MECHANIC
Yes, of course I loved him . . .
. . . I just wanted to protect him, and for a while I thought that I could . . .

When she doesn't say anything, he grabs her, shakes her.

Listen to me . . . Listen . . . There is not a night that goes by I don't dream that I catch him . . . I catch him in my hands before he hits the ground.
This makes her cry harder: she knows he is telling the truth. She looks at him, believing him, forgiving him now . . . He touches her face. She embraces him, feels the warmth from his body.

MECHANIC
We can start over . . . We can start over.

INT. *KRONOS*. FORWARD CARGO HOLD— DAY

Smilla and the Mechanic stand in the forward cargo hold looking into the strange cargo hold next to it.

SMILLA
What do you think?

MECHANIC
It's a receptacle for . . . for toxic waste.

SMILLA
Whatever it is they're picking up, it must be huge.

MECHANIC
It produces heat, melts the surrounding ice. Four men dived in the meltwater—and died within an hour of each other.
    Tørk and Loyen are under extreme pressure . . . they're gonna show no mercy . . . You can hide in my cabin, but only for a little while . . . The ship is approaching the coast . . . You'll have to go ashore. Okay?

EXT. *KRONOS*—DAWN

The Kronos now sails among giant icebergs, some of them bigger than the ship itself. On the horizon we see a thick white belt of field ice getting closer.

INT. *KRONOS*. CORRIDOR—DAWN

Only the dim night-light is on in the long dark corridor. The Mechanic and Smilla come out from the Mechanic's cabin. The Mechanic walks first as if to protect Smilla. They get to the companionway that leads to the cabins on the lower deck.

MECHANIC
I'll go down and get your things. You go up to Lukas—wait for me there . . .
And the Mechanic disappears down the companionway.

INT. *KRONOS*. WHEELHOUSE—DAWN

Smilla enters the wheelhouse. Lukas turns around. His eyes are more serious than ever. Then he continues to maneuver the Kronos *through the thick, dangerous field ice. Smilla stands for a while observing him, then tells him what she thinks he ought to know.*

SMILLA
They murdered your son, Lukas.
His eyes move away from the horizon. He looks at her.

LUKAS
You're lying. He's been placed in custody on the Nordic Star. He has a drug problem. I thought if I gave him a job, things would change.
Smilla steps closer to him.

SMILLA
They murdered him and left him to die on the pier. I was with him, I held him in my arms . . . I'm sorry.
He studies her. From the expression on her face he knows she is telling the truth.

LUKAS
Who killed him?

SMILLA
One of Tørk's men—Hansen.
Lukas looks out at the ice. His face is furious.

EXT. *KRONOS*—DAWN

A violent cracking sound as the stem of the Kronos *cuts through and breaks the thick field ice. It is early dawn; the sky is hanging bluish-black over the frozen sea. The* Kronos *sails along the coast now, which is completely covered with snow.*

EXT. *KRONOS*. DECK—DAWN

Deafening groans and creaks as the ship breaks up the ice.

from above. One last look between them and then Smilla lets go and falls heavily onto the ice as the ship continues moving past her.

Then, jumping across the open leads in the water, and knowing by the color of the ice where it will hold her weight, she makes her way toward the shore, a small figure buffeted by the terrible wind.

INT. *KRONOS.* UPPER DECK—DAWN

From his office window Tørk is watching Smilla through his binoculars.

INT. *KRONOS.* MECHANIC'S CABIN—DAWN

The Mechanic prepares his diving equipment.

EXT. GREENLAND. INLAND ICE—DAWN

Smilla begins the slow steady climb up the icy cliff. She is in her element, fearless. She looks out at the Kronos, which, like a small dot, works its way farther north through the ice. Smilla takes the map she stole from the upper deck out of a hidden pocket in her bag, reads "Gela Alta," and instead of going toward the small village now starts walking in the same direction as the ship.

EXT. GREENLAND. INLAND ICE—DAY

Smilla continues on, along a flat, windswept plateau crisscrossed with furrows as far as the eye can see. Using a probe, she pokes the snow in front of her, reading the ground before her as she takes every step.

Smilla in her Arctic clothes now, anorak and heavy kamiks, *stands with the Mechanic on the deserted deck. She is holding a rope attached to the railing.*

MECHANIC
Just go inland and wait for me . . . There's a village inside the bay, about seven miles to the south. *They embrace. And Smilla begins to lower herself down the rope to the bottom. Before stepping off, Smilla turns back to the Mechanic, watching her*

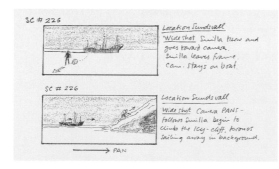

EXT. GREENLAND. INLAND ICE— DUSK

Smilla has prepared herself for the night by building a small primitive cave in the side of a glacier. There is a strong wind now, and the snow whirls around her.

EXT. GREENLAND. INLAND ICE. FJORD— DAY

Smilla comes walking, exhausted, on the edge of the inland ice. She holds the map in her hand. She stops, now seeing:
    Hundreds of feet below, resting at anchor in the fjord, amid thick plates of shattered ice broken up where it has pushed its way into the bay, sits the Kronos, *malevolent sentry in this astonishing landscape.*

EXT. GELA ALTA GLACIER—DAY

From a distance, through the swirling snow, Smilla can see the entrance to the man-made concrete tunnel that has been dynamited into the ice. There is an enormous door, propped open on huge pillars, where tracks have been laid, leading down into the bowels of a cave. Equipment rests all around the entrance.

INT. GLACIER. TUNNEL—DAY

Descending along the tracks that are used to ferry down the heavy equipment, Smilla makes her way hundreds of feet down the ice tunnel into the inland ice . . .
    Stops dead, gazing down in astonishment at what she sees . . .

INT. ICE CAVE—DAY

Below her is a cave: huge, stark, and sinister. A murky lake occupies the main area, filled with phosphorescent green water and lit with enormous halogen lamps, which create a thick haze in the air. In the center of the lake, half-submerged beneath the water, is a huge meteorite, its opaque gray surface pitted with craters, like a tiny moon. It is enclosed within a halo-like electron gyroscope like the rings around Saturn.

Smilla is standing at the tunnel entrance, fifteen feet higher than the level of the lake. Long trestle tables have been erected around the edge, laden with video monitors and electronic equipment hooked up to the gyroscope. There are tunnels leading off the lake to the right and left. Loyen and Tørk stand in front of the monitor.

Suddenly Smilla feels the mouth of a gun pointed against her temple. It is Hansen. Smilla does not budge. Tørk turns around, sees her, gives her an indulgent smile. He beckons her to come down to him. Smilla climbs down a short metal ladder leading to a perimeter ledge around the lake, which is screened off with tape.

Hansen follows her closely as she walks toward Tørk. She is mesmerized by the meteorite. Tørk shows her the monitor. The others have gone off to work, leaving them alone.

TØRK

I knew you'd come. For people with resources, the right events happen. They may look like coincidences, but they arise out of necessity.
Tørk hits a switch and the gyroscope starts to rotate, emitting a stream of electrons as it orbits the meteorite.

TØRK

Incredible, isn't it? We can see inside it. It is not a real meteorite . . . Meteorites are cold. This is

warm. Meteorites are dead. This is alive.

Smilla looks at the monitor: the tunneling electrons reveal layers of increasing density as we penetrate deeper inside the orbits of the meteorite. The energy seems to spin faster and faster as we reach the center—suddenly vanishing in a dark hole; and yet it is from this very dark hole that the energy is emerging.

Smilla looks at the surreal, glowing meteorite in the lake—then back at the monitor—this incredible creation of energy within the heart of darkness.

TØRK
Symmetrical energy, as it was in the beginning of time. You see how it's gathering energy from some sort of vacuum at the center.

This is the biggest scientific discovery of the century. Not just numbers on a piece of paper, or abstractions that take thirty years to be published in some obscure journal. But a stone that you can touch and feel . . .

SMILLA
You can't remove it and transport it to a densely populated part of the world. You could set off a catastrophe. If the worm was once widespread around the globe, its numbers were not limited until it had exterminated its hosts.

TØRK
Death is always a waste. But sometimes it's the only way to arouse people. Bohr participated in the construction of the atom bomb and thought it would promote peace.

When Smilla doesn't reply . . .

You lack imagination, Smilla, which is unforgivable in a scientist.

SMILLA
What about the boy? Why did Loyen examine him?

TØRK
He jumped into the damn water. He was afraid of heights, and we were forced to take him along into the cave. His father collapsed while he was still near the surface. The boy wanted to go to him. It was Loyen's idea to keep him under observation. The worm was subcutaneous in him, not in his internal organs. He never even felt it.

On a signal from Tørk, Hansen has come up behind her. He marches her ahead of him, turning on a headlamp and illuminating a tunnel in the cave.

INT. SIDE TUNNEL—DAY

A rectangular room, seven feet square. Smilla stops when she faces a wall of ice and turns to meet her death. Hansen raises the gun to shoot her. Then he lifts his feet off the ground, spreads his arms, rises a foot and a half in the air, and throws himself against the wall.

He hangs there, impaled like a giant insect against the ice, now crimson with his blood.

Lukas stands in the entrance to the tunnel holding a compressed-air harpoon. Lukas turns around and leaves, reloading the weapon as he goes.

INT. ICE CAVE—DAY

As Lukas moves toward Tørk, Smilla goes the other way, coming up behind Loyen.

Tørk is busy at the monitor. He has seen Lukas's reflection in it and turns to shoot him with a shotgun resting next to him. A dull blast and Lukas pirouettes and falls down on the ice.

Loyen is desperate, he grabs Smilla's arm, she tries to free herself, tumult—suddenly she manages to push him on the steep slippery ice and he falls into the green toxic meltwater.

Tørk is running toward her now, holding the shotgun in front of him.

The Mechanic has been working in the other tunnel, comes out at the sound of the shotgun and Loyen's screams. He is very surprised at seeing Smilla. Then he moves. He takes up an ice ax and throws it at Tørk, planting it in his arm.

Tørk drops his gun, pulls the ice ax out of his arm, and runs out through the tunnel, moaning in pain.

Loyen fights for his life in the lake but soon goes under in the ice-cold water.

EXT. GELA ALTA GLACIER. CAVE ENTRANCE—DAY

Smilla comes out of the cave and sees blood staining the snow. Smilla knows this is Tørk's blood, follows the bloody tracks away from the cave, toward the cliff leading down to the sea.

EXT. GELA ALTA GLACIER—DAY

Smilla continues to follow Tørk's blood, less of it now; she loses her way for a moment, finds the trail again, leading to the long slide down the glacier.

She continues on, almost at the shore now. There is no longer a trail of blood; she must use pure instinct now to follow him.

INT. ICE CAVE—DAY

The Mechanic attacks the top of a tank of compressed air for diving. Using a crowbar, he finally knocks off the top of the tank, revealing the detonator hidden inside. The canister is filled with plastic explosives. He turns the demand valve, which starts the timer, places it carefully on one side of the lake.

Suddenly Verlaine comes out of the tunnel, where he has just discovered Hansen, and tackles the Mechanic from behind. They both go down, slipping on the ice. The shotgun skitters away from both of them.

The Mechanic and Verlaine fight with their bare fists. A couple of blows and Verlaine is knocked unconscious.

The Mechanic runs to fix another oxygen tank. Sets the timer on this one as well.

Sc # 243-6 · INT. ICE CAVE - day

Medium shot as above. But the Mechanic reacts fast at turns the Dive bottle against the ice-stick, and stops it.

Sc # 243-7.

Close up of the Mechanics hand. Setting the timer.

Sc # 243-8

Medium close shot steady cam Seeing the Mechanic from behind. Verlaines POV. camera moves fast towards the Mechanic. M. turns around and stops the ice-stik

Sc # 243-9

Medium shot Verlaine knocks down the Mechanic to the ground. We see the dive-bottle rolling over the ground.

(ABOVE) *For shoots that demand a movable camera but where there is not enough room or where the ground does not allow the camera to move on tracks, a so-called steadycam operator is needed. He carries the incredibly heavy camera in its housing with a specially designed suspension to keep the camera—and the picture—steady as he runs alongside the actor. On* Smilla's Sense of Snow *the Swedish-American steadycam operator Mike Tiverios did the steadycam shootings*

EXT. GELA ALTA GLACIER—DAY

Smilla runs toward the ship's boat, sees Tørk trying to maneuver it out of the thick plates of ice. Tørk sees her approach and, unable to move, jumps from the boat and tries to get across the ice to the Kronos, anchored out in the bay.

Smilla follows him, both of them struggling against the wind and snow.

Ice floe: Tørk jumps from floe to floe; losing strength now, he arrives at a huge open lead. He leaps, misses by inches, his foot goes into the water—he struggles to pull it out and gain purchase on the ice, pulling himself up onto a floe.

Smilla stops suddenly, ten feet away. Tørk turns to face her. Smilla sees the blood pouring from a wound in his shoulder. He sits down on a big ice floe. He feels safe here where Smilla cannot reach him. Smilla stands on the solid ice only a few feet away from him.

SMILLA
The boy, Tørk . . . Tell me about the day he died.
Tørk is silent.

SMILLA
You were waiting outside his school, weren't you, Tørk? He's the only child who walks home alone.

EXT. STREET NEAR THE WHITE PALACE—DAY (FLASHBACK IN SLOW MOTION)

We now see what Smilla describes: Tørk follows Isaiah in his car, gets out, and grabs him by his sweatshirt. But Isaiah manages to free himself and runs away.

SMILLA (VOICE-OVER)
You grab him. Not by his arms, but by his clothes, so that you won't leave any marks. But you miscalculate.

EXT. GELA ALTA GLACIER—DAY

Tørk moves his weight from one foot to the other, causing the entire ice floe to rock.

SMILLA
He knows you, Tørk. Not just from the hospital, where you've spent hours tormenting him. But from the day he saw his father die. It's death itself he associates with you.

TØRK
You're guessing.

INT. WHITE PALACE. STAIRWAY—DAY (FLASHBACK IN SLOW MOTION)

Again we see what Smilla describes: Tørk running after Isaiah up the stairs. Isaiah knocks on Juliane's door, but there is no answer, so he continues up the stairs—and up the ladder to the hatch leading to the roof, all the time with Tørk right behind him.

SMILLA (VOICE-OVER)
He gets to his building, and then there's no escape. He knows what's behind him. He knows he's going to die. And this fear is even stronger than his fear of

Steadycam operator Mike Tiverios in action again—here on the roof of the White Palace

heights. Inside him an engine is spinning that will keep going until all his strength is used up.

EXT. FJORD. ICE FLOES NEAR SHORE—DAY

SMILLA
And you chase him up to the roof. Maybe for the first time it occurs to you not just to get the tape . . . but that it's possible to eliminate him . . .

EXT. WHITE PALACE. ROOFTOP—DAY (FLASHBACK)

SMILLA (VOICE-OVER)
. . . And avoid his ever telling anyone what he saw in a cave on a glacier in the Davis Strait.

EXT. FJORD. ICE FLOES NEAR SHORE—DAY

TØRK
I didn't mean to kill him. I needed the tape. He

panicked. I shouted . . . He turned around, but he didn't see me . . .

SMILLA
You're lying.

EXT. WHITE PALACE. ROOFTOP—DAY (FLASHBACK IN SLOW MOTION)

Isaiah is now on the roof—but so is Tørk. Isaiah runs across the roof toward the edge—Tørk just stands there watching him.

SMILLA (VOICE-OVER)
He didn't turn around. He couldn't hear a thing . . .
We see Isaiah spinning through the air as he falls toward the ground.

EXT. FJORD. ICE FLOES NEAR SHORE—DAY

Smilla looks Tørk straight in the eyes.

SMILLA
He was deaf.
They look at each other for a very long time.

EXT. GELA ALTA GLACIER. CAVE ENTRANCE—DAY

The Mechanic is hurtled out onto the snow as the door closes behind him, destroyed by the fireball from the bomb. The second bomb causes the enormous door to swing back open, throwing flaming debris high into the air. And the third causes the glacier itself to begin to move.

EXT. GELA ALTA GLACIER. SHORE—DAY

A terrible cracking sound. The ice groans and shrieks as it breaks away, and Smilla and Tørk both turn to see the glacier starting to calve off, huge

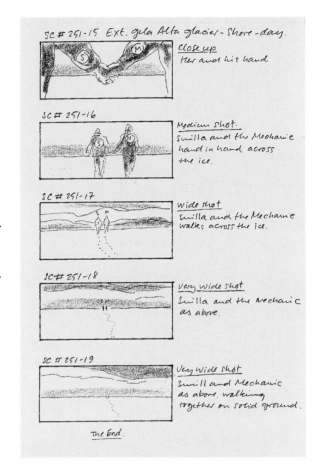

pieces of it falling into the sea below the cliff. Tørk realizes as he starts to move that he is heading out to sea on a fragile membrane of ice. He stands up, and that is when the first wave from the calving glacier hits them. He makes a desperate lunge toward the solid floe that Smilla is standing on, but the waves are too strong, and he falls into the water.

EXT. UNDERWATER—DAY

Tørk disappears from view.

EXT. GELA ALTA GLACIER. SHORE—DAY

Smilla watches as the Mechanic makes his way out toward her.
They stand for a while looking at each other. Her face is mild. Open. Serene.
He stands there facing for her. Has all the time in the world.
Then, slowly, she begins to walk toward him. She almost passes him, then stops.

SMILLA
You always follow me.

MECHANIC
I do my best . . .
She holds out her arm to him. He turns toward her and takes her hand, and then they walk, hand in hand across the ice, onto solid ground.

THE END

Part Three

Interviews with the Actors

Julia Ormond
(Smilla)

Interview with Karin Trolle

*H*ow did your acting career begin?
I decided to become an actress when I was eighteen. At that time I was just finishing school and already had a place at art school, so on completing that course, I applied to drama colleges in London. It was a time of great uncertainty, as you had nothing to compare yourself to, but the outcome was a place at Webber Douglas Academy of Dramatic Art, which I attended for three years.

After finishing drama school, I worked in repertory at the Crucible Theatre, Sheffield, and the Everyman Theatre, Cheltenham, and then went on to tour with the Manchester-based Royal Exchange Theatre Company. I made my London West End debut at the Garrick.

My first movie part came in Peter Greenaway's *The Baby of Macon.*
Do you have any worst or best memories of your career so far?
I wouldn't want to pick on a particular film, but I think the worst

Julia Ormond and Bille August concentrate on a long dialogue scene

moments have to have been where accidents have happened and people's or animals' lives have been put at risk and sometimes lost. It's easy to believe that you are somehow protected by the fantasy world of film; people are so eager to get it right and there's so much pressure timewise.

My first television role was as a heroin user in Channel 4's *Traffic*. Besides being a popular television program, this series was also shown in rehabilitation houses and to trainee customs officers. I still meet people who say that a member of their family or a close friend of theirs is a heroin user and that seeing the program either opened up discussion or helped them understand the problem better. I think that has to have been the best experience.

How do you usually prepare yourself for a part?

For me, the preparation for a part is an ongoing process throughout the time you live with that character. It's about understanding, experiencing, and immersing yourself in the world that character comes from. The research that you can do can stretch to infinity. Sometimes the hardest thing is to stop and trust your imagination and yourself. For me, preparation for a part is about building a base of

knowledge so that you can be free as the character. I always start by reading the text and talking to the director and, if possible, the writer. I then return to those areas of the text I don't understand and do the necessary research. Then you explore every aspect of that character's world: the politics, the climate—this affects the rhythm of a character; their clothing, which will affect the way a character moves; the period within which a piece is set, which will affect particular mannerisms; advancement of thinking. For example, did she think the world was flat? Much is dictated by the time setting. All of these things inform the makeup of a character.

Perhaps there are tasks that a character performs, or a profession demanding certain physical skills. It is normally just a matter of dedication and practice, but this can be hours of work. It's helpful to seek out somebody of the character's profession, talk to them, and observe them.

The physicality and the speech of the character are very important. One has to be careful to let these things grow organically from the story. None of it should be superficial. Costume is obviously something that's very important, as are hair and makeup. All of these are a statement of how characters express themselves in their present. It may be subcon-

scious, it can be conscious, but it's always a telling canvas. You have to be physically fit in order to bring energy and concentration to your work. From this foundation, I then work on finding the journey of the character through the text and finding how she relates to other characters. The text should give you answers to her psychological past which color her responses in the present. Then you have to trust that you have taken these things on board, let go of your own mannerisms and idiosyncrasies —and then you are free to improvise on the text.

Can you mention any more specific things you did in your preparation for the part of Smilla, which is in many ways a very demanding one? Smilla is a very special and strange woman from a very different country. You are in almost every shot, and there are many demanding fight and stunt scenes.

Before the shooting of *Smilla*, I was fortunately able to spend a lot of time with Bille August. We went to Greenland together, and he showed me around Copenhagen, going over the specific locations. We spent a good deal of time discussing the script and also Peter Høeg's novel on which the script was based. Going to Greenland was very important, as it is such an extraordinary place. It's where Smilla comes from and is a great source of motivation for her. We spent time talking to Inuits and Danish people living there. We went on dog sled rides, watched local singing and drum-dancing. We went to the local children's home and visited schools. We went out on the boats to see the icebergs and visited local museums. I visited places where the tradition of making the national costume is still carried on and visited the local markets. I watched the preparation of seal skins and talked to people about their hunting methods and the history of their culture. I took many photographs, not just of sights and people but of textures and colors.

In Copenhagen, I did a lot of reading, absorbed the culture there, visiting museums and galleries. We went to the Glaciological Museum and, in particular, the Greenlandic section of the National Museum. I met with glaciologists, both the people who worked in labs—observing them using equipment—and those who went on expeditions to Greenland. We were fortunate in finding someone who was female and Greenlandic. I spent a good deal of time with Marit Allen, who designed Smilla's costumes, and we discussed and found things that married Smilla's Greenlandic influence with her Danish side. We tested an enormous amount of costumes on camera, trying to find an expression of Smilla's individuality that wouldn't be distracting on-screen. Marit hunted down local Greenlandic and Danish designers of jewelry and clothing. With Gerlinde Kunz, who did the makeup, we tested several different looks and coloring to achieve a look that was natural but also Greenlandic.

I did a lot of physical training for Smilla because it was important to be very fit, not just because it was a hard and demanding shoot but because I am very sensitive to cold, and the fitter you are, the better you cope with that. We also did a lot of climbing at a local climbing wall so that I could do the stunts required, and we worked on the fight sequences with stunt coordinator Paul Weston. It was vital that these were accurate. Smilla suffers from hypothermia and burns during the course of the film, and I met with a doctor who treats both of these to discuss the physical symptoms and varying degrees of severity.

I worked with Penny Dyer, a dialogue coach, who spent a good deal of time tracking down someone with a similar background to Smilla so that she would have a similar sound. We worked together on all the Greenlandic words used in the text and on removing the Danish sounds from the accent. We then went into rehearsal. It's important that the sound is

Julia Ormond

English actress Julia Ormond studied for a year at the West Surrey College of Art and Design before training to become an actress at the Webber Douglas Academy. Stage work rapidly followed, and her London appearances include *The Rehearsal, Wuthering Heights, The Crucible,* and the Hammersmith Lyric Theatre production of Christopher Hampton's *Faith, Hope and Charity,* for which she won the 1989 London Drama Critics Award as Best Newcomer.

Ormond's film career includes an amazing range of roles. First she appeared in Peter Greenaway's *The Baby of Macon,* then in *Nostradamus* by Roger Christian. *Legends of the Fall,* directed by Ed Zwick, brought her international acclaim, and in *First Knight,* by Jerry Zucker, she plays Guinevere opposite Richard Gere and Sean Connery. In Sydney Pollack's remake of the Billy Wilder classic *Sabrina* she costars with Harrison Ford.

Other memorable performances came in HBO's *Stalin,* by Yvan Paffer; BBC's *Captives,* by Angela Pope; and TNT's *Young Catherine,* by Michael Anderson, for which she received a Genie Award nomination from the Academy of Canadian Cinema and

organic to the character: for me, it's something that isolates Smilla and yet keeps her connected to her roots. For me, that is Smilla's language and part of her character. We also found that it made sense of the moments when Smilla speaks Greenlandic.

I also met with the woman on whom Peter Høeg based the Greenlandic part of Smilla.

Could you say a little more about how you see the character of Smilla?

Smilla is an amazing character; not only does she embark on a great quest but her quest resolves something for her emotionally and spiritually. She is someone who is pushed through Isaiah's death to confront herself and her relationships with those around her. I believe that *Smilla's Sense of Snow* is also a profound and poetic piece, which is unusual in a modern drama. It was a great challenge for me.

I was also very interested in her independence and intelligence, her tenacity and her pain. She is someone who is geographically dislocated from her roots, who through her own integrity and willfulness is reducing her options of expression. She has a very objective view of the world and a dry sense of humor. She is very protective of herself, relating to snow, ice, math, and logic more easily than humans. She finds security in their reliability and has created her own philosophy from this. She has a dysfunctional relationship with her father and I don't believe has fully grieved over the death of her mother. Both Isaiah and, later, the Mechanic are people who break through her barriers and enable her to confront herself.

Smilla is very earthy and concerned about the abuse of the earth and its resources and, while accepting the cruelty of nature, is prepared to fight against human injustice, corruption, and ambition.

How did you like Greenland?

I loved Greenland! It's like the top of the world. The variety is surprising. When you fly over the glaciers and the ice cap, the snow and ice are like a white breathing skin, the contours constantly moving like a living thing. It is majestic, powerful, gentle, and peaceful all at once.

During your research for the part you met a number of Greenlanders both in Greenland and in Denmark. What is your impression of this people and their problems both in their own country and as immigrants in Denmark?

The Greenlanders are an indigenous culture who for thousands of years have found a way to live alongside nature, to respect it. They are a very expressive people, with extraordinary resilience. The young Greenlanders I met are particularly pro-Greenland, some studying in Copenhagen, longing to return. The Greenlanders who lived in Denmark varied a great deal in their response to the situation. To be honest, the only common denominator was that they all at some point had experienced prejudice.

Television in 1992.

After *Smilla's Sense of Snow,* Ormond went on to Russia to work on Nikita Mikalkov's *The Barber of Siberia.*

Gabriel Byrne

(The Mechanic)

Interview with Karin Trolle

When did you first know that you wanted to become an actor?
 I didn't want to become an actor. I didn't become an actor till I was about twenty-nine, which is quite old for somebody to start in that profession. But I had been teaching up to that time, and I did drama classes with the kids. From then I became interested in theater and eventually in film.

The first theater part I did had no lines whatsoever. I had to walk across the stage and just raise my hat and get out on the other side. Later I played the leading part in a play called *The Hostage*.

My first film part came with *Excalibur*, directed by John Boorman. He offered me a part after having seen me onstage in a play in Dublin.

Do you still do theater?

No, I haven't done theater for twelve years now. I prefer doing movies —always have. Of course, the direct contact with the audience can be exciting, but the immediate rapport between the audience and the stage is something that dies every night with the play. Some actors are addicted to it. I'm not. But I think that I may go back and do a play next year sometime, just for the experience.

What was it in the Smilla *script that made you accept the part?*

I read the novel about three years ago, and I really loved it. On the one hand it was a thriller and on the other hand it's an emotional story. I really liked all the characters. The character of the Mechanic is a mystery, an enigma, and to play a mystery or an enigma is difficult. I like that; you have to mislead the audience but you also have to make them believe in

Gabriel Byrne (the Mechanic) and Bille August in front of the Odd Fellows Mansion in Copenhagen, which served as the exterior of Moritz's club

you and at the same time doubt you. That's an interesting game to play. Because the Mechanic should be mysterious and most of him should be hidden, so that the audience doesn't quite know him. When he says to Smilla, "Don't you trust me?" and she looks at him and says, "No!" the audience shouldn't either. I find that very interesting, but I think it's the last kind of mysterious part I'm going to play. I've already played too many!

The Usual Suspects *for example.*

Yes, in *The Usual Suspects* I was also this secretive guy. So that's *it* now for mysterious parts.

This is not the first time you've been shooting in Denmark.

No, I did *Prince of Jutland*, too, with Gabriel Axel, and I had a great time doing that picture. A lot of really good actors . . . and Gabriel himself. I have really happy memories of Copenhagen. So I was glad to come back again and work in Denmark—and to work with Bille, whom I had already met in New York when he was casting *The House of the Spirits* a long time ago. We didn't work together that time, but I met him again in New York when *The House of the Spirits* came out. He is a very calm director. Very calm and logical. Never looses his cool, which is amazing on a film like this, because it was quite a difficult film from every point of view.

Did you like Greenland?

Greenland was amazing. It was a country I'd never been to before and I knew nothing about it. It was like being in the desert, except it was a desert of snow. And when you're in a wide-open space like that you feel that man is subservient to nature. You feel that you're really just a visitor. Everywhere else man has control of the environment, but not there. Yet at the same time you go into a supermarket and they've got compact discs and Disney toys. So it's a combination of the primitive and the twentieth century. It was really interesting from that point of view as well.

You're Irish, but you don't live in Ireland.

No, I live in Los Angeles. I have two kids, so I live there to be near them. But I miss Ireland. I have a house there and I still miss living there all the time. It's tough to live in America.

What is it that is so special about Ireland—this strong feeling Irish people have for their country?

I think a lot of it has to do with history and a lot of it has to do with the nature of the people themselves. We are a very friendly, hospitable, passionate, melancholy, witty, curious, introverted kind of people. We're all those things. And it's an incredibly beautiful but also very troubled

Gabriel Byrne

Gabriel Byrne started his acting career when he was nearly thirty. Up to then he worked as a schoolteacher in his native Ireland. He started at the Abbey Theater and later joined the Royal Court Theatre in London.

Byrne made his feature film debut in John Boorman's *Excalibur*. Other European films include the acclaimed *Defense of the Realm* and *Hannah K.* During this time Byrne worked for several noteworthy European directors, including Constantin Costa-Gavras, Ken Russell, and Ken Loach. In 1990, he made his American debut in the Coen brothers' film *Miller's Crossing*.

Since then, he has starred in Ralph Bakshi's *Cool World, A Dangerous Woman, Trial by Jury,* John Badham's *Point of No Return* and *Little Women.* He also starred in *The Usual Suspects* with Chazz Palminteri and Kevin Spacey and in *Frankie Starlight* with Matt Dillon. Most recently he played opposite Johnny Depp in Jim Jarmusch's *Deadman,* in *The Last of the High Kings,* which he co-wrote, and in *Trigger Happy* he stars with Jeff Goldblum and Richard Dreyfuss.

Smilla's Sense of Snow is the second film Byrne has made in Denmark. He also appeared in

country. However, the people are what make the country, and the people are really unique. There's nobody else in the world like the Irish. It is, of course, easy for me to say that, but the German people, for example, are in love with the Irish: Irish music, everything. And the Danes came to Ireland before anybody else, and they obviously knew where they were going. They knew it was a good place over there.

Playing the Mechanic, you had to stutter. Isn't it difficult to concentrate so hard on your language and still be able to concentrate on the rest of the acting? How can you do that?

Well, I used to stutter when I was a kid, so it wasn't anything that I had to think about. I don't really stammer anymore now, but sometimes when I'm very, very tired I can stammer a little bit. It disappeared by itself. I know people who've worked hard at it and it hasn't gone away. But I was lucky, I guess.

What do you do to prepare yourself for a part?

I just read the script a couple of times. And say the lines. Then wait for the director to say what's good or bad. But I think that the best thing is just to read the script as often as possible. I'm not really somebody who researches, because I believe that every role an actor plays is basically playing himself, even though most actors like to think that they're becoming somebody else. I don't think they are. I think they're just themselves. And whatever it is you have to play, it should come from inside you. Sometimes you need to learn about various things, but it mostly comes from inside.

Do you have a favorite movie?

I have a lot of favorite movies: Fellini's *Amarcord*; *The Four Hundred Blows*, by Truffaut; *Brief Encounter*, by David Lean; *Raging Bull* by Scorsese; *The Quiet Man*, by John Ford. A lot of favorite movies. I love a lot of Bergman's movies—not all of them, but I love *Fanny and Alexander*.

As an actor, you travel a lot, which means you're away from home for long periods of time. How do you maintain a close relationship with your children, your family, and your friends?

I try to work as little as I can, it's as simple as that. I have to work: I have to live; and I try as far as I possibly can to do films that don't take me away from home for long periods of time. *Smilla's Sense of Snow* is the longest film I've ever done, and for that reason I was somewhat ambivalent about doing the part, because it meant I had to be away from my kids for twelve weeks. I've never really been away from them for longer periods than three weeks at a time.

You know, I think that anybody who works in the movie business works very hard, and people pay a very high price for being in movies; a very high price which I don't really want to pay. Because I don't think that any movie is really worth the price of what people have to give up.

Danish director Gabriel Axel's *Prince of Jutland*.

Byrne devides his time between writing, producing, and acting. He was executive producer on Jim Sheridan's film *In the Name of the Father,* which earned several Oscar nominations, including Best Picture, and he also produced and starred in *Into the West,* opposite Ellen Barkin. His first book, *Pictures in My Head,* was published in December 1995 in Ireland, where it became a critically acclaimed bestseller. The book was published in America in September 1996.

Richard Harris

(Tørk)

Interview with Karin Trolle

Y*ou started your acting career in the theater?*
 Yes, I trained in the theater, trained in the classics. Studied at the London Academy of Music and Dramatic Art.
 Do you prefer doing theater or movies?
 You can't compare the two. When I do theater I love doing theater, when I do film I love doing film. I have the same enthusiasm for both. But I haven't been onstage for four years. Not since *Henry IV*.
 Of course, it's more challenging doing theater. Every night is a challenge because things can go wrong. In a movie you can keep doing it until you get it right. And then the director can cut around it . . . make you look better. Onstage it's just you, just you by yourself, so therefore there's an immediacy about it that makes it far more challenging, and more exciting.

 Which of your parts did you like the best?
 I think *Henry IV*, the one I did four years ago, was my favorite theater part, and of film parts I think *This Sporting Life*. Actually, the two films I was nominated for an Academy Award as Best Actor, *This Sporting Life* and *The Field*, are my two favorite movie parts.
 You have told me that when you were offered the part in Smilla, *you*

didn't know Bille August and you weren't sure if you were going to accept
the part of Tørk.

That's true. I didn't know Bille August. I don't go to movies anymore.
But I told my son who's a director in Hollywood about this offer, and he
said, "Well, who's the director?" and when I told him it was Bille August
he said, "Then you have to do it. You must do it." I told him it was a small
part, but he said, "It doesn't matter, you have to do it." So I accepted the
part for several reasons.

A. Because of Bille.

B. Because of Julia Ormond. I'm a fan of Julia's since I first saw her in a movie on the life of Joseph Stalin where Robert Duvall played Stalin, and I think she was absolutely brilliant.

And C. The script is very intriguing.

Also—to be honest with you—it mattered to me that I only had to work eight days over five or six weeks, so I have had all this time off. Spencer Tracy used to make hit movie after hit movie; everything he did was successful. So people thought he must have some kind of secret formula as to how to choose scripts that were all so success-ful, and they said to him, "When you read a script, what do you look for?" And he said,

Richard Harris (Tørk) and Bille August on an ice floe in Greenland

"My days off." At my age, I can't do a lot. I mean, I can't do a fifteen-week picture anymore. I'm not interested in that.

But in spite of your age you did some rather extraordinary stunts your-self in Greenland on this movie. You went into the water in Ilulissat, Greenland, in March. Even though you were wearing a dry suit it was quite an accomplishment.

Madness. I was mad. I was stupid to do it. But I did it . . . I think the Irish have that urge for challenges. We jump to a challenge . . . And it looks good on the screen.

How do you see Tørk as a character?

You don't really know anything about him. Of course, he's the "bad guy" in the story, but he's not an evil man. Only he is a scientist and as such very curious, very ambitious, and very determined to obtain what he's after. Also, he's a very greedy man. Not greedy for money, but greedy for acknowledgment and fame. And somehow the little boy gets in his way.

But it was a very uncomplicated part for me to play. There was no preparation for this part at all. For some pictures it takes a long time. For my part in *The Field* it took me about four, five months before we started shooting—just preparing it. I did a wonderful movie two years ago with Robert Duvall called *Wrestling Ernest Hemingway*. It took months of preparation.

Bille August directs Richard Harris

Studying the character, how he's going to walk and talk, all that. But for some parts you don't need it, and Tørk was one of those parts.

Is that because some characters are closer to yourself than others?

Yes, and because some parts are more complicated than others. But one big error the young actors do is that they overcomplicate things. I heard about a young actor who was going to play a fireman in New York. He worked for months in a fire department. I mean, do you think that Spencer Tracy, when he played a cop, went to join the police force? Not at all. They overcomplicate things. I've studied Method acting in England and I'm not a believer in it.

Many of the Actors Studio actors make everything too personal. They

Richard Harris

Richard Harris appears in *Smilla's Sense of Snow* as the ambitious and determined scientist Tørk.

Born in Limerick, Harris studied his craft at the London Academy of Music and Dramatic Art, making his London stage debut in Joan Littlewood's 1956 production of Brendan Behan's *The Quare Fellow*. His West End reputation was established with *The Ginger Man*. Among his early feature films are *The Guns of Navarone* and *Mutiny on the Bounty*, but it was Lindsay Anderson's film of the David Storey novel *This Sporting Life* that propelled him to international stardom. His portrayal of the angry young rugby football player won him the Cannes Festival Award as Best Actor and an Oscar nomination.

Among his countless film appearances since then are Antonioni's *The Red Desert*, *Camelot*, opposite Vanessa Redgrave, Elliot Silverstein's *A Man Called Horse*, and *The Wild Geese*, by Irvin Kershner. More recently he has been seen in Clint Eastwood's *Unforgiven*, Phillip Noyce's *Patriot Games*, and Darrell James Roodt's *Cry, the Beloved Country*. His bravura performance as an Irish farmer protecting

don't share the emotions with you. They're cocooned in a cell of their own character and don't listen when the other actors speak. They're too busy in their own world to communicate. I find it very self-indulgent and rather boring.

When you travel as much as you do, how do you maintain your relationships with family and friends?

Very, very difficult!

I've divorced twice because of that. It's best not to have a deep, solid relationship. It's much better. It's very difficult to make love long distance, over the telephone. It's impossible. It's easy for me now, because I'm older and my kids have grown up, so there's not that pressure anymore.

You're Irish. Do you live in Ireland?

No, I don't, but I go back a lot. I love Ireland. It's a passion. I love and absolutely adore Ireland and the Irish. I wouldn't want to be from anywhere else.

I used to have a house in Ireland and a house in England, but the income tax people put a stop to that. So now when I go back to Ireland I rent a house there or I stay at hotels. But my house, my actual home, is in the Bahamas. I'm hardly ever there, but I collect paintings and they're all there.

Most Irish people talk about Ireland the way you do. What is it about Ireland that makes it so special?

It's when you travel the world that you realize that it's unique. The Irish are terribly generous. They have a fantastic outlook on life. Like it's today, it's now, there's no such thing as tomorrow. People who worry about tomorrow don't live today. It's a wonderful philosophy: it's all happening now. And they generally believe that today is not a rehearsal. Today is it. There will never be a May 23, 1996, again. That's how they live. And they're very passionate. They're very fiery and they're very forgiving. You wouldn't think that because of their politics. You'd think they're unforgiving—because of their conflict in Northern Ireland. But they *are* forgiving. They just don't like being taken advantage of. When you think that England has been in Ireland for six hundred years and they never conquered the Irish . . . They occupied Ireland, but they never beat the Irish spirit. That's why today we're an independent republic. They couldn't beat the Irish spirit and they never will.

Then there's the culture of Ireland. Think of that tiny little island—and we've got four Nobel prizes in literature. We've had Bernard Shaw, W. B. Yeats, Samuel Beckett, and now Seamus Heaney. Four Nobel laureates. Not bad. If you could sculpture the soul of Ireland it would be a work of art.

Do you intend to continue acting as long as you can, or do you have any plans for retiring?

I don't know. Every time I decide to do a picture I say that it'll be my last. Then I do another one. You know, the fire I used to have is going out now. The fire in my stomach, the fire in my heart for acting . . . these past two years it has begun to dwindle.

his property in *The Field* won him a second Academy Award nomination.

Harris recently added writing to his accomplishments and is the author of a novel, *Honour Bound*, and a collection of poetry, *I in the Membership of My Days*.

Robert Loggia
(Moritz)

Interview with Karin Trolle

*H*ow did *your acting career start?*

I was attending college on a football scholarship, and a professor asked me if I wanted to be in *The Taming of the Shrew*, which I did. I realized that it was safer and certainly a lot more fun to be onstage than on the football field. I got my degree in journalism. Then I went into the army, and on getting out of there I decided I wanted to be an actor. I started working right away. Two weeks after I got out of the army I got a job on Broadway. I've always worked as an actor and I've never had to do anything else. None of that stuff of waiting at tables or all that junk. I've been very fortunate in my career. I've done a lot of theater—on Broadway, off Broadway—and I've done a lot of television series. I was a member of the Actors Studio. I was a very serious actor, I developed my craft and I'm glad I did, for I've never been afraid of acting like those people who achieve a certain fame but have no technique. They are afraid of getting old because then they don't know what they'll do. I'll probably die on a stage—somebody will have to play Grandpa and that might as well be me.

So you have no plans of retiring?

No. I talked with Richard Harris about this—we've known each other for twenty-five years. Of course, his hair is white now, although I'm a year older than he is—I'm sixty-six and he's sixty-five—but he looks like Grandpa to me. Anyway, we were saying that if you're an actor and not worried about getting older and playing your age, you can have a good life. You travel all over the world; it's great fun: especially if you're not carrying a picture. This film is a perfect example: a wonderful script, Bille is a great director, you come to Denmark, and, hopefully, you've helped. Then you move on to another job—it's a good life.

Do you prefer working in the theater or in films?

I prefer film now. But I don't think you can become an actor with a technique—at least in my generation—unless you've worked on the stage. And also worked on pieces by the major playwrights: Chekhov, Strindberg, O'Neill, Tennessee Williams. You have to have that in your storehouse, because if you have played those roles—if you have played Jean in *Miss Julie*, as I have—then it's not too difficult to play Moritz in a movie.

Bille August with Robert Loggia between takes

Your first movie part was in Somebody Up There Likes Me *in 1956—forty years ago, and as you say, you've done a lot since then. Do you have a favorite part?*

I got an Academy Award nomination for *Jagged Edge*, so of course that was important. I loved doing *Scarface* with Al Pacino. When you work with good actors like Pacino and Julia Ormond it is very enjoyable. I've done my own television series, too, but I sort of enjoy the surprise of not knowing what's around the corner, so I haven't really enjoyed doing television series very much, because it is too much of the same thing. I like the unknown. That's fun.

You accepted the part as Moritz at very short notice. Isn't it difficult to prepare yourself in such a short time?

No, not really. Well, I wish I had read the novel first, which I hadn't,

Robert Loggia

Robert Loggia plays Smilla's father, Moritz.

Rarely absent from the cinema or television screens, Loggia has a career spanning more than forty years, making him one of the most familiar faces on the international entertainment scene.

Loggia's list of television films and series credits is extremely long. He received an Ace Award nomination for Best Actor for his portrayal of renowned defense attorney William Kunstler in HBO's *The Trial of the Chicago Eight*, and the series *Mancuso F.B.I.* earned him an Emmy nomination as Best Dramatic Actor.

Loggia's first film role, in

and I would have liked to come over here at least a week ahead of time— it's not easy struggling with jet lag and having to start work immediately, so in that way it was difficult. But I found Bille August such a gentleman, so nice. He really helped me. I feel I've made a friend; I'm really fond of him. And even if it was at short notice I wanted to do the part because I knew Bille August's work and I really worship Julia Ormond—I think she's certainly among the top five actresses in the world today. And the rest of the cast: Richard Harris, Vanessa Redgrave, Gabriel Byrne . . . I was glad to get a chance to be in such a great company.

How do you usually prepare yourself for a part?

It depends on the part. In *Scarface* I played a Cuban drug dealer, Frank Lopez. He spoke with a Cuban accent, and we rehearsed that for three weeks, so that took a good deal of preparation. To play something that's close to you—like playing the father of Smilla—is not that difficult. I have three daughters, so in this case my life was my preparation.

Can you relate to Moritz's guilty conscience as regards Smilla?

I think that every parent has a guilty conscience with their kids. They feel they could have done better. There's usually some conflict with children . . . certainly with mine. I got divorced and then remarried, and for the children that's a very difficult situation. Life is not easy for any of us. That's one of the reasons why I think this picture will touch people. They will identify with Smilla, who is very much a searcher: searching for happiness, security, whatever that means. This picture is dealing with universal emotions.

Moritz does his best. He was in Greenland, he fell in love with this

Inuit woman, they had a child, his wife died, and now he wants to come back to Denmark, but the child wants to stay. She's at home in Greenland and he forces her to come back. The child is untamed. She's used to the wide-open spaces, it's her culture, so he has a problem. She's always getting thrown out of schools and all that. But Moritz is not a bad person. He's trying to deal with his own life, has a new relationship with Benja, who is jealous of Smilla because she reminds Moritz of his Inuit wife. So it's difficult for Moritz to stand between these two women. But he does what he can—and tries to buy his way out.

Do you have a favorite movie?

I never get tired of *Casablanca*. Ever. I think I could watch it every day. It's a picture which is a total accident—I know the history of the picture. But somehow *Casablanca* is what film is all about.

You played with Ingrid Bergman in A Woman Called Golda?

Yes, she played Golda Meir and I played Anwar Sadat. We had a good relationship, I was fortunate to make her acquaintance. We became good friends. I said goodbye to her only a couple of weeks before she died. That was in her home in England. We talked for a few hours, said goodbye. She was a great lady.

Do you still do theater?

Not too much. I was offered the musical *Victor Victoria*. It was to be a two-year run, and I said no. I hate to get off the wheel of movies. It's exciting. My wife and I get to travel a lot. The children have grown up and the world is our oyster.

1955, was as Paul Newman's costar in *Somebody Up There Likes Me*. A memorable collection of character roles followed; his Anwar Sadat to Ingrid Bergman's Golda Meir, in 1981, attests to his chameleon-like talent.

During the 1980s Loggia became one of Hollywood's leading character actors, his work at this time including a unforgettable performance in *An Officer and a Gentleman* and a rousing piano dance with Tom Hanks in *Big*. In 1986 he received an Academy Award nomination for his part in *Jagged Edge*. He also turned in memorable performances in such films as Brian de Palma's *Scarface*, John Huston's *Prizzi's Honor*, and John Schlesinger's *The Believers*. His impressive talents were most recently on display in the part of General Gray in the action science fiction film of 1996, *Independence Day* by Roland Emmerich.

Agga Olsen
(Juliane)

Interview with Karin Trolle

*F*or someone who was born and raised in Greenland, and still lives there, acting hardly seems the most obvious choice of profession, does it?

No, it doesn't, but ever since I was little I've wanted to be an actor. I've been treading the boards since my Girl Scout days. As a child I also sang in the church choir, at christenings and the like, and I've been singing onstage since the age of fourteen as a rock singer and backing vocalist. I've always loved performing, and fortunately for me there were scores of amateur-dramatic groups in Greenland back then. Things really were humming in my hometown, Sisimiut, what with amateur dramatics and pop groups. But of course I first had to get myself an education, so I took this two-year Greenlandic teacher training course that was on offer at that time. After that I taught for three years at a school in Nuuk. Then the Tuukkaq Theatre Company visited the town and I saw my chance. I applied for a place with the company and two weeks later received word that I had been accepted. I moved to Fjaltring in Denmark, where the company was based, in 1980 and was on the road for the greater part of my training period. It was tough as well as great fun, and I learned a lot.

What kind of theater was this?

Greenlandic pieces. Mask and drum dance and experimental theater. At that time Tuukkaq ranked fifth among drama schools in Denmark, but it's closed now. The drama school was moved to Nuuk in Greenland, and since we had already completed our training we formed our own theater group, the Silamiut Theater Company, of which I am a founding member. We've staged masses of productions, plays for children in particular. And we've recorded a whole lot of songs: children's songs, love songs, and political songs.

Had you done any film work prior to Smilla?

Yes, I had. With my looks I've played a lot of drunks and a lot of mothers. I also made an information film for Alcoholics Anonymous which was shot in Iceland and Greenland. And I played the part of "Mother of the Sea" in a children's film, acting alongside some marvelous Greenlandic child actors. That was in 1991.

I know that children in Greenland call you something other than Agga. Does this name stem from that part?

No. I had cut back somewhat on the time I spent on tour and applied for a job with a teacher training college, where I ended up teaching drama for six months. Then a job came up with the Greenlandic KNR-TV, who needed someone to make their children's programs, and since I had some small experience of the film world I got the job. I did children's programs for two years. That was when I created Atsa Rosa, a weird and wacky auntie-type character

whom all the children love. That was a wonderful time, but it was also a very lonely time. You become very isolated when you're writing scripts yourself, and producing, and all the rest of it. You miss having someone to bounce things off.

Then just at the point where I was running out of ideas, Bille August came to town and I attended your auditions in the hope of getting a small part. And I was in luck.

But the part of Juliane is anything but small. Did you find it hard playing such a major role opposite an actor as experienced as Julia Ormond, for example?

I got on well with Julia. We didn't get in each other's way and I knew I couldn't bombard her with lots of questions. I think that we were both quite at ease and we felt comfortable with each other; we both knew we were professionals. It's a tough part to play, but that didn't stop us from having a bit of a laugh now and again. And I met some wonderful people. Never in all my life have I met such an efficient bunch of people. Everything went like clockwork. I felt very much at ease.

And Bille was of great help to me. I've never worked with a director like him before, so calm. You never see him looking stressed. You'd hardly know he was there. Working with him was a tremendous experience, and I hope he'll have need of me again sometime.

How do you feel about the part itself? Can you understand the way Juliane reacts, the way she behaves toward the boy?

No, personally I can't. It's difficult to get under the skin of that woman. I mean, you just don't treat your child like that. Of course, a writer is free to create such a person and, unfortunately, such people do also exist in real life, but as far as I was concerned it was pure fiction.

How did you prepare for "getting under the skin" of Juliane and portraying her so vividly?

I did some research. I lived with a woman who was having a pretty bad time of it. I think I've grasped how some people can be so far gone that they will, in fact, abandon their own child. And, as an actor, once you've done your preparation for a part, been made up, donned that woman's clothes, and find yourself in her chaotic apartment, then you assume her identity, then you become "Juliane."

What was it like to have to work with a child who has some trouble concentrating on the matter in hand?

Well, in fact, I only had one scene with him, and in that he is lying on the ground, dead. I wouldn't have minded working a bit more with him, as his mother—I kind of missed that. But you know, we did become tremendously close friends, because we were living next door to each other in the hotel and sometimes I looked after him for his father. We had a lovely time, we went to the amusement park Bakken and to the Experimentarium. I miss that little boy very much.

As a Greenlander, how do you react to the fact that some of the Greenlandic roles, the boy, for example, and Smilla, too, were—for various reasons—played by non-Greenlanders?

The thing is that in a big-budget film such as this you *have* to have a number of professional and well-known actors. I don't think there's anything strange in that. What I *do* hope is that people will now realize that there are also some very gifted Greenlandic actors around, with the courage and the talent to tackle big projects.

Has this given you the courage to appear in more films?

You'd better believe it. I'm going home now to work on a Finnish film in which I've been given a small part, and which we'll be shooting in August. But I would like to do freelance work and I hope I'll be able to pick up some work here in Denmark. I've been considering moving down here to live, but that probably won't happen until next year, since I'm also just about to start directing a show in Nuuk: a musical entitled *Arnajaraq*. It's opening in the new cultural center there in February 1997. Directing is an exciting business, too.

How do people in Greenland feel about an international, non-Greenlandic film crew coming up and "taking over" their town—in our case Ilulissat?

They were thrilled—especially when they heard that Richard Harris was in the cast. He's a big star. Everybody remembers him from *A Man Called Horse*. They've all sat and wept over that film. And everyone tells me, "Say hello to Julia, say hello to Richard Harris," and so on. And those people who were directly involved with the film are very proud of their contribution to it, not least because of all the press coverage the film has been getting. We hope the world will have its eyes opened to Greenland—both culturally and in terms of tourism.

Clipper Miano
(Isaiah)

Karin Trolle

Clipper is seven years old and, like most boys of his age, more interested in playing or kicking a soccer ball around than in talking to a grownup. I first met Clipper at a costume fitting before shooting on *Smilla* got under way. He turned up with his dad and his brother, who is one year his junior, and the two boys were high as kites—pretty hyped up over this new and exciting situation in which they had suddenly found themselves. I have to admit thinking to myself, "How on earth is this ever going to work?" But, as it turned out, Clipper knew quite well when things were "for real," when it was time to concentrate. Both at our morning meetings in his trailer, where we would run through his lines for the scene to be shot that day, and during the actual takes, he managed to maintain concentration for *just* the amount of time required (but not a second longer!). And it did no harm, either, to have an extremely patient director with a great deal of experience of directing children.

Clipper comes from Toronto, Canada, where he is in the second grade at the Sacré Coeur School. He speaks both English and French—and sometimes a delightful mixture of the two. His "acting career" began when some people from the Toronto production of *Miss Saigon* visited his school to cast child extras for the show. Clipper was among those chosen and appeared in fifty-six performances over the course of the following six months. He then went on to make a number of commercials for, among other things, kitchen appliances, toothpaste, and cars. Clipper is now on the books of an agency specializing in child actors, and it was through this agency that we found him and chose him to play the part of Isaiah.

To my question as to what Clipper enjoys about acting in the theater and in films he replies that he likes playing a part. He also thinks it is fun to travel and to spend long periods of time in another country—except for the fact that he often has an upset stomach because the food is different from that at home. Not surprisingly, he finds all the hanging about between takes boring.

I ask Clipper whether he misses his mother and the rest of his family (he also has a new baby sister), but no, he doesn't. There are too many exciting things going on around him, and besides, he speaks to his mother regularly on the telephone. He has also sent her a postcard, he announces proudly. And then,

Bille August explains to Clipper how he must run up the stairs, terrified, in the scene where he is being chased

In the airplane on the way back from Kiruna, Sweden, Julia Ormond and Clipper Miano have fallen asleep. It is obvious that they are good friends

his father, Pascal Miano, goes everywhere with him. Pascal is a schoolteacher, but has taken a sabbatical to be with his son during filming.

What Clipper enjoys most are his days off. While in Copenhagen he has visited both the amusement park Bakken in Dyrehaven park to the north of the city and Tivoli, and has also spent a lot of time in a video games arcade called Fun House where there is one machine with cuddly toys as prizes. At this point his father interrupts to say that he has had to buy an extra suitcase in which to carry home all the cuddly toys Clipper has won.

Clipper was not on the Greenland shoot, but since we needed to film one scene of him playing in the snow with Smilla, he did come with us to Kiruna. Clipper was not too happy about being there and, once again, the food was one of the main sources of complaint—this evidently being a subject of great concern to our young actor. In Sweden, the only dish that was to his taste was *köttbullar* (Swedish meatballs) and he thought the french fries were particularly poor. Nonetheless, he does have a couple of good memories of his stay in Sweden. He rode on a dog sled and tried steering a *sparkstøtte*—a special sort of sled propelled by pushing off with one foot, as with a child's scooter.

Being absent from school for so long does not worry Clipper in the slightest. Nor should it, since he has his dad, the schoolteacher, right on hand. Pascal does, in fact, give his son lessons every day when they are away from home, to prevent him from falling behind in his school work.

The person on the shoot to whom Clipper has become most attached is Julia, who understood just how to build up the rapport between them essential

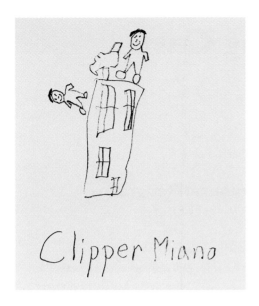

Clipper Miano

Clipper's storyboard for the scene where he falls off the roof. The man on the roof is Bille August with the camera

for their scenes together. Clipper tells me that he has drunk hot cocoa in her trailer on several occasions; he has even spent a night at her home.

One of the takes Clipper remembers best is the very first scene he had to do, where he is sitting crying under the stairs. A couple of days earlier he had gone for a costume fitting and tried on the clothes he would be wearing. He then turned up on the set and went to put on the clothes again, only to find that in the meantime they had become dirty. Isaiah had to look neglected and very grubby, so the clothes had been messed up a bit and there was dried jam on the T-shirt. Clipper found this too disgusting for words, and the dresser had to bring all her powers of persuasion to bear before he could be talked into putting it on. He also had vivid memories of the scene in which Smilla gives Isaiah a bath. This scene had to be redone nine times in all, and when it was over, Clipper confided to me that he wouldn't need to take a bath for the next nine days.

Clipper cites *Beethoven*, *Free Willy 2*, and *Toy Story* as his favorite films.

When I ask Clipper whether he would like to make more films, he has no hesitation in replying, "Yes, because then I can make more money."

217

Supporting Cast

*Bille August and
Vanessa Redgrave*

Vanessa Redgrave

(Elsa Lübing)

In *Smilla's Sense of Snow* Vanessa Redgrave plays Elsa Lübing, who helps Smilla, as she literally holds the key to the mystery surrounding the death of Isaiah. This is the second time Vanessa Redgrave has worked with Bille August, the first being the part of Nivéa, Clara's mother, in *The House of the Spirits*.

Vanessa Redgrave comes from a remarkable acting family. Daughter of Sir Michael Redgrave and his actress wife, Rachel Kempson, she is the sister of actors Lynn and Corin Redgrave. Actresses Natasha and Joely Richardson, her daughters by the late Tony Richardson, continue the dynasty.

Vanessa Redgrave has had an outstanding stage career in Britain and the U.S.A. She has appeared with the Royal Shakespeare Company and starred in many productions in London's West End and on Broadway, including Tennessee Williams's *Orpheus Descending*, winning a rapturous reception on both sides of the Atlantic, *Antony and Cleopatra* and *Vita and Virginia*. She is presently starring at the Royal National Theatre with Paul Scofield and Eileen Atkins in Henrik Ibsen's *John Gabriel Borkman*.

Vanessa Redgrave made her film debut in 1958 with *Behind the Mask* by Brian Desmond Hurst, and highlights since then include Antonioni's *Blow-Up*, Karel Reisz's *Morgan: A Suitable Case for Treatment*, Fred Zinnemann's *A Man for All Seasons*, Joshua Logan's *Camelot* (with Richard Harris), and Ken Russell's *Isadora*. Her title role in *Mary, Queen of Scots* by Charles Jarrott won her an Academy Award nomination, an honor she eventually won for her performance in *Julia* by Fred Zinnemann.

Recent films include James Ivory's *The Bostonians*, with Christopher Reeve; David Hare's *Wetherby*; *Little Odessa*, with Tim Roth; James Ivory's *Howards End*, with Anthony Hopkins and Emma Thompson; *A Month by the Lake*, with Edward Fox; and Brian de Palma's *Mission: Impossible*, with Tom Cruise.

The list of awards and nominations won by Vanessa Redgrave is very long and impressive, including several Academy Awards, Golden Globe Awards, Cannes Film Festival Awards, and Emmy Awards.

Jim Broadbent

(Lagerman)

British actor Jim Broadbent plays the pathologist Lagermann, who is mysteriously removed from the autopsy on the boy Isaiah.

After having studied at the London Academy of Music and Dramatic Arts, Broadbent worked at the National Theatre, the Royal Shakespeare Company, and provincial theaters. Among the plays in which he appeared are *As You Like It*, *The Tempest*, *Twelfth Night*, *The Family Reunion*, *Every Good Boy*

Deserves a Favour, *The Greatest Story Ever Told*, and *The Winter's Tale*.

Broadbent's career includes a great number of television films and series, and he appears in such outstanding movies as Brian Gibson's *Breaking Glass*, Terry Gilliam's *Time Bandits*, Mike Newell's *The Good Father* and *Enchanted April*, Mike Leigh's *Life Is Sweet*, Neil Jordan's *The Crying Game*, Michael Austin's *Princess Caraboo*, and Woody Allen's *Bullets over Broadway*. His most recent films include *Richard III* by Richard Longcraine and Christopher Hampton's *Secret Agent*.

Peter Capaldi

(Lander)

Scottish actor Peter Capaldi plays the Mechanic's friend Lander, who

helps Smilla to get on board the *Kronos*.

Capaldi's short career has been dynamic and covers both sides of the camera. His work for the cinema includes lead roles in *Local Hero*, *Soft Top, Hard Shoulder*, and *Lair of the White Worm*, in addition to a noteworthy performance in Stephen Frears's *Dangerous Liaisons*.

On television, Capaldi has been seen in *Prime Suspect 3*, among many other top series.

Capaldi recently turned to directing; his adaptation of Franz Kafka's *It's a Wonderful Life* won him the 1994 BAFTA Award for Best Short Film.

Emma Croft

(Benja)

Moritz's young girlfriend, Benja, is played by Emma Croft, who is regarded as one of the most promising comers on the British entertainment scene. She trained at the London Studio Centre, winning the award for Outstanding Drama Student in 1988.

Croft's theater work for the English Stage Company includes the West End and touring productions of *Coriolanus* and *The Winter's Tale*, both for director Michael Bogdanov. Other stage work includes productions for the Theatre Museum and Drama Academy.

On television, Croft has been seen in such popular series as *The Governor, Ruth Rendell Mysteries—Master of the Moor, A Dark Adapted Eye*, and *Snow*.

Before flying out to Scandinavia for *Smilla* she completed the film *Suede: Introducing the Band*. Other screen credits include *Kleptophilia, The Fifth Day*, and *As You Like It*.

Tom Wilkinson

(Loyen)

British actor Tom Wilkinson portrays Loyen. He recently appeared in the award-winning BBC TV series *Martin Chuzzlewit*. Other TV work includes guest lead roles in *Inspector Morse, Prime Suspect*, and *Resnick*. Other memorable TV work for the

BBC includes *Measure for Measure*, *A Very Open Prison*, and *Eskimo Day*.

Wilkinson's theater work includes the role of John Proctor in *The Crucible* at the National Theatre, Lear in *King Lear* in the West End, and Dr. Stockmann in the award-winning production of *An Enemy of the People*.

Since 1976 Wilkinson has appeared in a number of films, among them Andrej Wajda's *The Shadow Line*; Jim Goddard's *Bones*; Danish director Gabriel Axel's *Prince of Jutland*, with Gabriel Byrne; Barry Devlin's *All Things Bright and Beautiful*; Jim Sheridan's *In the Name of the Father*, also with Gabriel Byrne; and he played Father Matthew in Antonia Bird's *Priest*. In Ang Lee's *Sense and Sensibility* Wilkinson played Mr. Dashwood, and he also appears in *The Ghost and the Darkness*, by Steven Hopkins. Two forthcoming films in which Wilkinson appears are Gillian Armstrong's *Oscar and Lucinda* and Brian Gilbert's *Oscar Wilde*.

Bob Peck

(Ravn}

Leading British actor Bob Peck plays the part of Police Inspector Ravn.

Peck perfected his craft on the stage, including several years with the Royal Shakespeare Company, for which he played many classical roles, among them Soliony in *The Three Sisters*, Hastings in *Richard III*, Malvolio in *Twelfth Night*, Sir Mulberry Hawk in *Nicholas Nickleby*, Caliban in *The Tempest*, the title roles in *King Lear* and *Macbeth*, and Iago in *Othello*.

Another notable performance was the part of Rutherford in the National Theatre production of *Rutherford and I*.

Peck's numerous television appearences include parts in Jim Goddard's adaption of *Nicholas Nickleby* and Martin Campbell's series for the BBC *Edge of Darkness*, for which Peck won the BAFTA Best Actor Award and the British Press Guild Prize in 1985.

Most recently Peck has costarred with Ed Harris in *Parker*, and played the part of Muldoon in Steven Spielberg's *Jurassic Park* and Gilot in Merchant-Ivory's *Surviving Picasso*.

Mario Adorf

(Captain Lukas)

Captain Lukas of the *Kronos* is played by the German actor Mario Adorf.

Though born in Zurich, Adorf has made his career in Germany, studying at the Falckenbergschule in Munich before joining the Munich Chamber Theater.

Adorf's most important theater parts include classics by Tennessee Williams, Beaumarchais, Molière, and Shakespeare, and in 1979 he was awarded the Hersfeed Award for his performance as Arturo Ui in Brecht's play.

Adorf's film career took off when he won both the State Film Prize and international recognition with his portrayal of mass murderer Bruno Ludke in Robert Liodmak's film *Nachts, Wenn der Teufel Kam* (*The Night the Devil Came*). Since then he has made more than a hundred

feature and television films in and outside Germany, including *Don Camillo and Peppone* and *Smiley's People* for the BBC, Sam Peckinpah's *Major Dundee*, Billy Wilder's *Fedora*, Claude Chabrol's *Quiet Days in Clichy*, Fassbinder's *Lola*, and Schlöndorff's *The Tin Drum*.

Jürgen Vogel
(Jakkelsen)

On board the *Kronos*, Smilla makes a friend, Jakkelsen, played by young German actor Jürgen Vogel.

Most of Vogel's work for stage and screen has been done in Germany, where his films include Egon Günther's *Rosamunde*, Claude Oliver Rudolph's *The Wonderbeats*; Sönke Wortmann's *Kleine Haie (Little Sharks)*, which won him the Bavarian Film Award and the National Film Award and a nomination for the European Film Award in Geneva; Rainer Kaufmann's TV movie *Under Duress*, for which Vogel won the Civic Prize and the Telestar Award for Best Actor; Mathias Glasner's *The Mediocrities*; Dani Levy's *Stille Nacht*; and Mathias Glasner's *Sexy Sadie*.

After *Smilla's Sense of Snow*, Vogel went on to prepare a new film by Mathias Glasner, *Some Dead Bodies*.

Lars Brygman

(Verlaine)

Tørk's right-hand man, Verlaine, is played by Danish actor Lars Brygman.

Born in Denmark in 1957, Brygman first worked as a carpenter but later decided to become an actor. He took private acting classes and since 1987 has appeared on-stage all over Denmark.

Brygman has also acted in a number of television features and in films produced at the Danish Film School. In 1996, he received a Danish Theater Award for a monologue performed in a play entitled *Flugten* (*The Escape*).

Erik Holmey

(Hansen)

Hansen, one of the "villains" on board the *Kronos*, is played by Danish actor Erik Holmey.

Holmey trained to be an actor from 1969 to 1972, going on to work at the Royal Danish Theater for two years. Since then he has performed at theaters throughout Scandinavia, and his credits include *Cabaret*, by Masteroff; *The Sunshine Boys*, by Neil Simon; *Longboat*, by Frans G.

225

Bengtson; *Troilus and Cressida*, by Shakespeare; and *Irma la Douce*, by Heneker and Norman.

Holmey has appeared in a number of Danish and international movies and television features such as *Conan the Barbarian, Conan the Destroyer, Tukuma* (a film about Green land), and *Red Sonja*, where he doubled for Arnold Schwarzenegger.

Peter Gantzler

(Maurice)

Another of the "bad guys" on board the *Kronos*, Maurice, is played by Danish actor Peter Gantzler.

Gantzler attended the National Theater School from 1986 to 1990 and has since appeared in a great number of plays at Danish theaters.

He has also appeared in major Danish TV series such as *Kald Mig Liva* (*Call Me Liva*) and *Mørklægning* (*Blackout*) and plays the main character in a forthcoming TV movie, *Taxi*. Peter Gantzler's film credits include Lone Scherfig's *Kajs Fødselsdag* (*Kaj's Birthday*).